# QUALITY FIRST INVESTING
## A CHECKLIST APPROACH TO FINDING AND SITTING TIGHT IN MULTIBAGGERS

**BJÖRN FAHLÉN**

"This is a treasure trove of practical insights on how to understand the qualitative dynamics and future potential of a business!"
– *John Mihaljevic, Chairman MOI Global*

The author provides this book for your personal use only. You may not make it publicly available in any way. *Copyright infringement is against the law.*

Information and opinions presented in this book have been obtained or derived from sources the author believes to be reliable, but he makes no representation as to their accuracy or completeness.

The book's advice and strategies may not be suitable for your situation and should not be considered as investment advice of any form. You should consult professional advisors, including investment, legal and tax advisors, prior to making any investment decisions on the basis of the information contained herein. Neither the author and publisher, nor Redeye AB or its subsidiaries, will be liable for any loss or other commercial damages, including but not limited to special, incidental, consequential or other damages. Past performance, such as the performance of the investment strategies described in this book, does not guarantee future results.

Copyright © 2021 by Björn Fahlén

All rights reserved.

ISBN: 9798780728245 (Paperback)

ISBN: 9798787283235 (Hardcover)

Published in the United States by Kindle Direct Publishing

*This book is dedicated to Redeye's equity analysts and other independent thinkers who commit to undertaking the deepest bottom-up fundamental research on companies.*

# CONTENTS

| | |
|---|---|
| About The Author | 9 |
| Preface | 15 |
| Introduction | 25 |
| Acknowledgements | 29 |

## PEOPLE TENETS

| | |
|---|---|
| Background | 33 |
| Business Passion Analysis | 36 |
| Execution Capability Analysis | 48 |
| Proxy Guide: Corporate Strategy | 61 |
| Capital Allocation Analysis | 68 |
| Investor Communication Analysis | 87 |
| Executive Compensation Analysis | 102 |
| Proxy Guide: Compensation Basics | 113 |
| Ownership Strength Analysis | 116 |
| Board Leadership Analysis | 127 |

## BUSINESS TENETS

| | |
|---|---|
| Background | 143 |
| Business Scalability Analysis | 145 |
| Market Structure Analysis | 156 |
| Value Proposition Analysis | 171 |
| Competitive Moat Analysis | 185 |
| Proxy Guide: Competitive Moats | 199 |
| Operational Risk Analysis | 204 |
| Social Responsibility Analysis | 215 |

## FINANCIAL TENETS

| | |
|---|---|
| Background | 233 |
| Earnings Power Analysis | 235 |
| Profit Margins Analysis | 246 |
| Growth Rates Analysis | 260 |
| Financial Health Analysis | 272 |
| Earnings Quality Analysis | 295 |

## BRINGING IT ALL TOGETHER

| | |
|---|---|
| Time Favours Quality Investing | 307 |
| Patience Pays Off in Investing | 312 |
| The Redeye Top Picks Portfolio | 323 |
| Closing Words | 341 |

## APPENDIX A: CHANNEL CHECKS

| | |
|---|---|
| How to Conduct Your Channel Checks | 349 |

## APPENDIX B: DISCOUNT RATE

| | |
|---|---|
| Estimating the Discount Rate | 357 |

## APPENDIX C: VALUATION

| | |
|---|---|
| Redeye's Valuation Approach | 365 |

## APPENDIX D: QUALITY CHECKLIST

| | |
|---|---|
| People | 373 |
| Business | 380 |
| Financials | 386 |
| Index | 391 |

# ABOUT THE AUTHOR

## MY TRANSFORMATIONAL JOURNEY AS AN INVESTOR

Before you decide to invest all or part of your life savings according to my advice in this book, or even just to commit a few hours of your valuable time to reading it, some flavour of who I am and what experiences have shaped me may be in order. I'm talking both as a human and as an investor since the two seem to be interlinked.

When I was about 11 (back in 1986) I was surprised to catch my headmaster father watching TV intensely in the daytime. This was highly unusual. It wasn't a show, just numbers on the screen [Text-TV]. I asked him what he was doing. He told me he invested his carefully saved money in stocks.

"If these numbers go up, I will have made money," he explained. "Without doing any work?", I asked. "Exactly." I was fascinated. Making money without actually working? Total freedom.

At the time I was a paperboy. It was my first real experience of hard work providing money to get me what I wanted. The main reason I took the job was that I wanted to buy my first computer. After I saved up for that, a Commodore 64, I was ready to move to the next level – saving to invest. I had a separate savings account for party and travel, which I funded from working in peat bogs and IKEA warehouses.

I started out investing in mutual funds in 1989, when I was 14. As I learned more, my investments did fairly well and I started to gain confidence. Due to the good results I had with my fund picks, I thought I could pick individual stocks too. My first two were the pharmaceutical companies Astra and Pharmacia – partly due to both my beloved grandmothers having passed away due to cancer.

At this time, by when I was about 20, I was truly bitten by the investment bug. This is what I am going to do in my life, I told myself. And it was. While I was right about one thing when it comes to stock investing, I was wrong about the other. Being an investor involves a lot of freedom. But not without doing work. Lots of work, in fact – but fun work.

In my early 20s I studied chemical engineering, economics and business administration at university. From there I moved on to a biochemistry Ph.D. program, in part because of my family history of cancer. I was interested in cancer research. The biotech sector became my main circle of competence until I was about 30. From there it expanded into medtech, diagnostics and life science tools as I started my career as an equity analyst.

My first phase as an investor was in the biotech field, looking for stocks with good potential for extremely high returns. I usually invested heavily ahead of data releases or drug approval. After some missteps in the biotech bubble of 2000 I almost lost it all.

From that hard-earned experience I developed a biotech investing strategy. This was to take the initial stake off the table right before the roulette wheel stopped spinning to risk just my gains. Typically, in these special situations expectations rise as the event approaches and we see a surge in price – so there were typically gains to risk.

Combined with a stop-loss at 20% below my purchase price it was a good strategy in theory. I thought I had figured out how to beat the casino. Indeed, the strategy was fairly successful at first. But when combined with leverage and an extremely concentrated portfolio of three to five stocks it became a deadly cocktail in 2007-2008, when the stock market tanked.

As the financial crisis unfolded, I came close for a second time to being wiped out. I froze up with dead stocks in my portfolio that I thought were too cheap to discard. The lesson I learned cost me millions, in any currency, but I loved it too much to give up. This was a turning point in my life as an investor as it sent me back to the drawing board. Of course, the stock market acts like a casino, but only for those who treat it like one. After thinking deeply about the process of investing I began to focus on high-quality growth stocks instead of 'hope stocks', as the former typically come back strongly after market crashes. Moreover, high-quality growth stocks, also called compounders, tend to do very well in bull markets too. So why gamble when you have a formula that works?

Experience comes with age, no doubt. There are no shortcuts there I'm afraid. The truth is that you just have to make your mistakes to develop a resilient investment strategy that works for you. Most investors start out as casual investors. But selecting shares is not a casual experience to be undertaken lightly. Successful investing in the stock market over time requires discipline, patience and a proper strategy. The latter takes time and experience to develop.

Trial and error is the best way of moving forward and failure is the road to success. Fail early and fast and you will find success much quicker – but only if you admit and learn from your failures. In my case I almost lost it all early on when I did not have much to lose and I learned some hard truths along the way. This was critical for my mindset at that time, but it's certainly not a recipe for everyone.

While we all have different paths to knowledge of the stock market, reading a wide range of authors can save years of hard lessons paid from your capital. One of the books that truly opened my eyes and empowered my investing strategy was *One Up On Wall Street* by Peter Lynch. It taught me how to process a growth opportunity and create my own investment strategy.

Another investor that had a huge influence on me was Philip Fisher, who emphasised great, fast growing businesses with substantial untapped potential rather than bargain stocks. His book *Common Stocks and Uncommon Profits* was a lightbulb moment for me. I also have to mention Howard Marks' *The Most Important Thing*, which opened my eyes to the importance of a contrarian mindset and gave deep insights into market cycles. I try never to miss a memo of his at Oaktree Capital.

Lastly, the two books that influenced me the most are *100 to 1 in the Stock Market* by Thomas Phelps and *100 Baggers** by Christopher Mayer. They both studied the characteristics of companies that have delivered 100-fold returns for their owners. The latter was inspired by Phelps' work and published as a follow-up book, drawing from and extending Phelps' insights. Together, they opened my eyes to the strategy of investing in companies with lots of room to expand and the potential to vastly outpace their peers and sticking with them as long as the thesis is intact, even when they reach lofty valuations – holding on to let the power of compounding do its work.

> * The term multibaggers was coined by Peter Lynch in his 1988 book *One Up on Wall Street* and comes from baseball where 'bags' or 'bases' that a runner reaches measure each play's success. For example, a ten bagger is a stock which gives returns equal to 10 times the investment over a long period of time, while a hundred bagger stock gives a return of 100 times.

The books mentioned above have undoubtedly changed my life as an investor for the better. Other books that have influenced the way I invest are from authors focused on behavioural investing – in particular, Crosby, Greenblatt, Montier, and O'Shaughnessy. When it comes to decision making and probability, I think of Duke, Portnoy and Taleb. Finally, when it comes to biographies I must mention Baid, Schroeder and Spier as their books preach a holistic approach to investing – aiming to compound knowledge, goodwill and relationships, not just money.

Speaking of writers, Nobel laureate William Faulkner once said: "There is no mechanical way to get the writing done, no short cut. The young writer would be a fool to follow a theory. Teach yourself by your own mistakes; people learn only by error. The good artist believes that nobody is good enough to give him advice. He has supreme vanity. No matter how much he admires the old writer, he wants to beat him."

What Faulkner says holds true for investing as well. Everything I have learned about investing I have learned by doing, by making my own mistakes. Sometimes these were painful and even devastating, as mentioned. But they provided priceless lessons all the same.

Nobody in the industry has ever taught me directly how to invest. Instead I studied others' approaches and read countless of books, reports and articles; I discussed investing with colleagues and friends; and most importantly, I invested my own money. Blending all this together I have created my own investment philosophy, which you are about to dig deeper into.

As an investor you are in the business of acquiring wisdom. This is my contribution. Please enjoy and benefit from it.

Björn Fahlén

# PREFACE

## WHAT THIS BOOK COVERS

This book aims to help you systematically evaluate any company's quality via a structured checklist of questions. It explains the methodology behind Redeye's quality rating system, highlighting the characteristics that make companies more likely to prosper over time and those that can hinder them. It is primarily <u>a practical guidebook to quality investing through in-depth, on-the-ground research</u> – a continuing process of testing reality.

The assessment is based on a set of clearly defined fundamental criteria that seeks to identify companies of outstanding quality. Both soft and hard criteria like management's character and capabilities, the sustainability of competitive advantages and balance sheet stability are considered – all key factors in its future profitability. However, some factors may be more attributes of performance, rather than drivers of it.

These aspects are often time-consuming to discern and the analysis isn't always clear-cut. But this is where true value lies. Anyone with average intelligence, curiosity, time and a good internet connection can do it. Still, you must enjoy the work involved in the analysis process as it is essential to your investment success.

The key to success in the stock market is to <u>systematically evaluate every stock</u> from as many angles as possible before buying. In carefully running through this checklist the goal is to develop a deep understanding of the investment. This helps you to manage risk through knowledge as it allows you to see not just where things are but where they're going. This will help you tell quality companies from mediocre ones <u>by asking the important questions</u>.

When you apply the checklist to any company, you are trying to answer three key questions:

1. Does the business have great people behind it?
2. Does the business have favourable long-term prospects?
3. Does the business have solid financial fundamentals?

Good questions are the foundation for developing deep understanding and reliable evaluation. They lead to more powerful questions by refining your thoughts and helping you refine your inquiry. Basically, the questions in the checklist will help you to avoid things that don't work and seek out good businesses, run by good people. Of course, no businesses will get an entirely clean bill of health across all questions.

Some of the questions might be deal-breakers for you while others may require trade-offs, but that's up to you to decide. Personally, I seek to avoid running the checklist with much higher weightings for some questions than others. I prefer to run it without any bias and analyse what comes out of it.

As we quantify the checks, we're able to make relevant comparisons and sound judgement calls while also heeding Keynes' wise words: "It is better to be roughly right than precisely wrong." However, just as two people will hardly ever interpret a piece of art the same way, they will rarely derive exactly the same rating scores.

A low score doesn't mean that an investment will fail, any more than a high one guarantees success. But heeding the scores should shift you towards buying high-quality companies, which will help reduce your investment risk. Moreover, it will help you to act rationally and unemotionally when facts do not justify action. For example, many investors and analysts who do extensive research on a company have a strong bias towards buying or recommending the stock, even if their conclusions might not fully support it, to avoid having 'wasted' their time.

Note that this book is not about day trading. Likewise, if you're focused on what the business will produce in the next quarter or the next year, this book probably isn't relevant to you.

## WHY USE AN INVESTMENT CHECKLIST

An investment checklist reduces the emotional dimensions of investing and helps you see blind spots you may have ignored. Typically, you apply it as a last step before making an investment to verify that nothing has been missed. It usually takes no more than 30 minutes to run if you know the business very well. It will highlight-issues that you should go back and do some more research on. It forces you to seek out contradictory evidence that you may have overlooked or need to look at again to assess the likelihood of those issues causing problems. Then you can try to weigh them in your mind to determine whether they negate the benefits of the investment.

Less experienced investors can use the checklist as a starting point for the entire research process from which to gain a deeper understanding of the business and its people. This is something that makes your bottom-up fundamental analysis more consistent, but also typically more time-consuming. However, it's hard to be an intelligent owner of a business unless you have considered all these checks or similar ones. If you go in without deep knowledge of the business, you are playing a game of chance and your investment outcome will be more based on luck. Knowing too little is obviously dangerous, but knowing too much can also be dangerous if it forces attention away from what matters.

Basically, the purpose of an investment checklist <u>is about avoiding what doesn't work and seeking what does work from your own and others' experience</u>. As a result, you don't need to invent the wheel each time you research a stock, but rather just follow the lessons and mistakes of the past. Of course, you must also avoid falling into a 'check the box' mode, as this will impede your high-level goal of gaining insight on durability and value.

A checklist also grounds you. Your confidence in the case should rise when you go over the checklist. While doing the necessary research, you get a better understanding of the company's merits and shortcomings. It increases your chances of success and reduces the risk of suffering a loss. When you feel your chances have gone up as you get more knowledgeable about the business, you naturally will feel more confident in the investment and more comfortable maintaining conviction in the face of uncertainty. But keep in mind that it takes time for some fundamentals to crystallize. Your conviction will only strengthen when your knowledge about the company is confirmed and management delivers on its promises.

Nonetheless, stay alert to the potential for a false sense of security from using the checklist. Never forget that there are always risks that we cannot prepare for.

## WHO THIS BOOK IS FOR

I sincerely hope this book offers both new and more experienced investors useful ways of refreshing their filters in the search for great companies. Though it is possible to work through the book without any business training, a basic understanding of company accounting and valuation would be helpful. So, this book is not aimed at beginners, but is rather aimed at <u>more experienced investors</u> who study company fundamentals and want to improve their research process. They typically manage their own stock portfolios or are professional long-term investors.

However, a second group of readers for this book is <u>senior managers and directors</u> who are willing to roll up their sleeves and get into the details of how great companies create long-term shareholder wealth. The words and actions of the people behind a business can sometimes be very profitable, while they can also destroy value – sometimes overnight. It pays to understand the difference.

More than anything, this is a book for people who are independent thinkers and are confident in trusting their own judgement. They are likely to be <u>people who are ready to invest significant amounts of time in doing the necessary research</u> – those who stick to what they know, know what they own, and think about it more consciously. As the technology entrepreneur and investor Peter Thiel famously once said, "The most contrarian thing of all is not to oppose the crowd but to think for yourself."

## HOW THIS BOOK IS STRUCTURED

The framework of this book is a checklist based on a set of quality checks across three tenets: PEOPLE, BUSINESS and FINANCIALS. These are the building blocks that enable companies to deliver sustained operational outperformance and attractive long-term earnings growth.

Each tenet is grouped into separate categories assessed by six checks. The first three parts of this book explains the three tenets in detail, along with why each quality check matters and how to assess it. Note that all of the checks fail by default when you are unsure or when disclosure is insufficient.

Some say that smart people learn from their own mistakes while wise people learn from the mistakes of others. To me, the goal is to be both smart and wise. So I've slowly built this checklist over the years, responding to my mistakes and learning from those of other investors.

No doubt useful questions are still missing and some may seem to be duplicates. However, it remains a proven, practical tool – one that has been the key success factor behind the Redeye Top Picks Portfolio, which has delivered returns of 436% over the past five years (as of 15 November 2021).

We come back to this in the final part of the book, 'Bringing it all together'. This explains how you can and why you should incorporate this under-explored investment philosophy into your own investment process.

You can read the final part in its entirety before the rest of the book, as it sums up the arguments of why quality is the key to successful investing and why you need to develop a deep understanding of the business behind the stock. The latter is of the outmost importance to finding the courage to sit tight as the stock goes up ten or even hundred times. Finally, you don't have to read the whole thing. It's okay, just follow your curiosity and interests.

## PART 1: DOES THE BUSINESS HAVE GREAT PEOPLE BEHIND IT?

Part 1 is all about people and identifying trustworthy leadership, or at least avoiding companies led by people of questionable character. The point is that you should trust management if research suggests they are trust-worthy, and then work hard to verify that trust. Businesses' success is driven by people. It doesn't matter how great a company's product is if management doesn't make the right decisions. You want to invest in companies that are run by people who bring an owner's perspective to their role and are focused on delivering long-term shareholder value.

I once read a story about the importance of a trustworthy management. It can be summarized something like this: what's your money really worth if you put some of it in a safety locker that you don't have access to and the fellow who does is a crook?

If you invest in a great business run by incompetent, crooked or dishonest management or owners, you may benefit for a while. However, over time you will end up regretting your decision.

Once you understand how critical the people who run the company are to a successful outcome, you will have greater success as an investor. Poor leadership may do well in the nearer term, but in most cases will affect the company like gravity over the longer term. The business eventually follows management back down. Yet assessing the calibre of management teams is no easy task.

The checklist for People is divided into seven categories: *Business Passion, Execution Capability, Capital Allocation, Investor*

*Communication, Executive Compensation, Ownership Strength,* and *Board Leadership.*

## PART 2: DOES THE BUSINESS HAVE FAVOURABLE LONG-TERM PROSPECTS?

In Part 2, you will learn how to find companies with a compounding growth outlook, namely a resilient business model with a long runway to grow. Knowing the business model inside out will provide you some level of certainty and reduce the risk when you buy a stock. Furthermore, it should provide you an edge over other investors in assessing where the business will be in the future, its operational risks, its direct and indirect competitors, and the likelihood of it succeeding.

The checklist for Business is divided into six categories: *Business Scalability, Market Structure, Value Proposition, Competitive Moat, Operational Risks*, and *Social Responsibility.*

## PART 3: DOES THE BUSINESS HAVE SOLID FINANCIAL FUNDAMENTALS?

In Part 3, you will learn how to evaluate a business's financial soundness through a few key financial ratios. Financial ratio analysis will be useless if you lack the knowledge to interpret the numbers or simply take financial statements at their face value. Moreover, this kind of analysis is only worthwhile if it produces actionable insights.

It is the qualities of the business and its people that ultimately produce the quantitative results. By the time you see the quality in the financial ratios, the share has probably already seen its steepest rally.

The checklist for Financials is divided into five categories: *Earnings Power, Profit Margin, Growth Rate, Financial Health* and *Earnings Quality*.

## PART 4: BRINGING IT ALL TOGETHER

Investors quite commonly feel that they need to score frequent home runs to compound wealth at a high rate. But this is not necessarily the case, as you will see in Part 4.

Buying high-quality companies without paying premium prices is just as much value investing as buying companies of average or poor quality at discount prices. Quality is systematically underpriced by markets over extended time periods. Strategies that exploit the quality dimension of value can be profitable on their own, and accounting for both dimensions of value yields dramatic performance improvements over traditional value strategies.

High-quality companies tend to be expensive, while cheap stocks tend to reflect companies of low quality. It follows that quality strategies are short value, while value strategies are short quality. Consequently, each strategy tends to do well precisely when the other underperforms, making them highly attractive to run together. Combining these two strategies achieves a two-dimensional margin of safety, as you improve your chances of handling the inevitable challenges like bad luck, bad timing, and bad judgement.

<u>The bottom line is that high-quality companies bought at a low – or even a fair price – typically provide superior returns over time.</u> High-quality investing is not just less risky, it also delivers a better return on time invested than buying cheap stocks of poor quality. Furthermore, holding investments with unrealised gains over the long term is often tax-efficient.

## APPENDICES

In the Appendices you will learn tactics for gaining little known facts about companies that can give you an edge in investing. This involves gathering small pieces of non-material information from people who are closer to the company or more knowledgeable about its industry than you and piecing these together to form a material conclusion. The point is to pick up information other investors aren't likely to.

Once a company has been selected for its exceptional qualities, a realistic valuation of its intrinsic value has to be approximately assessed. You will learn how to determine what is a reasonable price at which to invest in that company, and how Redeye incorporates the key concept of business quality into the discount rate we use in valuing companies. However, the book doesn't go into the detail of building company valuation models as that would be beyond its scope.

Finally, the complete checklist is provided with all questions, to be used as an overview or as a scorecard for your own research.

## TERMINOLOGY

Throughout this book I use the term 'product' to cover the broadest possible range of manufactured products and services.

I also treat the terms 'stock' and 'share' as interchangeable.

I use 'profit' rather than 'earnings' where possible to avoid possible confusion with revenue measures.

# INTRODUCTION

The average investor focuses way too much on 'the forest' and not enough on 'the trees', in my opinion. There is too much focus on the economy or where interest rates or the markets are going or what the impact of the election is going to be. Most of this is unknowable. This focus on the now is a distraction from the long-term fundamentals. I believe <u>investors would be better off if they focused on understanding businesses and how to think about them</u> – the focus of this book.

Knowing how to invest is an essential skill of life. While a formal education gives you the tools to earn an income, it rarely tells you how to make your money last and keep it from running out before you do. Nobody in the investing industry ever taught me much, directly, but I learned a great deal about investing by doing, watching and reading pretty much every book on investing I could get my hands on. I have learned a lot about investing along the way and am glad to be able to share my experience with you here.

This book began as a small internal project at Redeye AB, a Stockholm-based boutique investment bank founded in 1999. The project's initial scope was to institutionalise lessons learned from refining the equity research process during my many years as an equity analyst and investing in the stock market. This book illuminates the way to the path of long-term wealth for you and your heirs as it will teach you how to pick companies wisely.

What I have come to understand is that <u>quality is the key to successful investing</u>. If you are a long-term investor, it's hard to find a more important factor among those that power your ultimate investment returns. Buying great companies at good prices tilts the probability of success in your favour. While luck plays a disproportionate role in whether you make money from valuation alone, it typically doesn't when it is combined with an assessment of quality.

The bottom line is that <u>quality of the business comes first and valuation second</u>. The idea here is that not losing money is the best way of making money. You should always spend more time thinking about the competitive position and long-term prospects of the business than worrying about whether the stock price happens to be cheap at the moment. Valuation is unquestionable a critical input in the decision-making process, but it should not be the starting point.

As Benjamin Franklin once said, "The bitterness of poor quality remains long after the sweetness of low price is forgotten." Focusing on the quality of the business will help you to avoid pitfalls and mistakes that drag returns down.

If you want to be a great investor, you need to be systematic and strategic in how you analyse companies. Over time I gradually came to see the patterns of what constitutes a high-quality business – predictability with the potential to compound over a long period of time. This book is my attempt to codify a framework for analysing businesses' quality – one of the most complex processes my career has exposed me to.

Going through the checklist described in this book for companies you are considering as investments will empower you with knowledge and understanding about them that less diligent investors will not be aware of. It doesn't matter whether you copy the checklist or customize it to your own needs, as long as it improves your analysis process.

Quality is dynamic and changes over time, as very few businesses continue to be successful for decades. Moreover, quality is challenging to measure with precision because it often involves more subjective qualitative factors than easily quantifiable measurements. Nonetheless, in making decisions we tend to pay too much attention to readily available numerical metrics and relegate quality as it typically doesn't have a numerical score. After all, it's often easier to explain that a stock is cheap than that a company is great.

Finally, you're better off putting a lot of effort into a few great companies than a little energy into many. Developing a deep understanding of companies' qualitative dynamics and future potential is probably the greatest source of advantage you can give yourself as an investor.

In other words, there is no substitute for knowing your investments inside out – or at least better than most so you can develop the conviction to hold them and the knowledge of when to sell before the majority. As Peter Lynch says, "in investing, the person that turns over the most rocks wins the game."

*Happy compounding!*

Björn Fahlén
November 15<sup>th</sup>, 2021

# ACKNOWLEDGEMENTS

I particularly need to doff my hat to John Mihaljevic, chairman of MOI Global and managing editor of The Manual of Ideas. He inspired me to publishing my writings about the subject as a book.

For invaluable input, special thanks to my colleagues at Redeye; to Henrik Andersson, fund manager at Didner & Gerge Fonder and co-founder of InvestingByTheBooks.com; and to Peter Edwall, investor and founder of Odin Asset Management.

I would like to thank Julian Lewis, editor extraordinaire. He reads my stuff and polishes it to a high gloss after many challenges over diction, paragraph structure and chapter organisation.

Also, I would like to thank Jesper Wiking who created an outstanding book cover. The koi fish symbolises wealth and success in China. Moreover, it is known for its ability to swim against the current and travel upstream – just as great investors do.

Lastly, but also firstly, my wife, Maria, has been highly supportive of this publication by relieving me of many duties that might have interfered with it. Thank you.

Bless you all!

# PEOPLE TENETS

## DOES THE BUSINESS HAVE GREAT PEOPLE BEHIND IT?

# BACKGROUND

At the end of the day, people drive profits. Not numbers. Understanding the motivations of people behind a business is a significant part of understanding the long-term drive of the company. It all comes down to doing business with people you trust. Trust in management is paramount in smaller companies, but still very important when investing in large caps.

I've learned over time that great management teams deliver positive surprises and bad ones negative surprises. And few high-quality companies have weak management. Conversely, poor businesses typically have the effect of repelling both good management and good owners.

When it comes to people, the best predictor of future behaviour is past behaviour. Accordingly, you should judge management by what they do, not what they say. By not rushing into investment decisions and by taking the time to understand a management team, you can reduce your risk of misjudging them.

Most errors in assessing managers are made when you see only what you want to see and ignore flaws or warning signs.

For example, always avoid CEOs who hire compensation advisors with expertise in what can be accomplished legally to their benefit and appoint friends as patsy directors who will permit the abuse of outside shareholders.

Two of the biggest mistakes you can make as an investor are to blindly trust management statements and to ignore signs of poor corporate governance standards. You should take seriously even the slightest doubt over these key areas. That's why we have incorporated the quality of the board into the assessment of a management team. Directors hold the keys to arguably the two biggest controllable factors in a business – compensation and capital allocation.

## THE FRAMEWORK

The People rating is based on quantitative scores in seven sub-categories: *Business Passion, Execution Capability, Capital Allocation, Investor Communication, Executive Compensation, Ownership Strength,* and *Board Leadership.*

All of these sub-categories are assessed on five quantitative and qualitative checks. Each is allocated one point if the question can be answered positively; the total number of these points makes up each sub-category's score on a scale that ranges from 0 to 5, rounded to the nearest whole number. If unsure about a question or disclosure is inadequate, the check fails by default. This is consistent with the best ideas often being the simplest.

Each sub-category also includes a sixth complementary check. These negative questions provide additional information to assist with investment decision-making, but have no impact on the scoring model.

## ESG ANALYSIS

To fully understand companies' long-term prospects the checklist also covers ESG issues. Analysing these factors is central to measuring the sustainability and ethical impact of an investment in any company. We address the E (environmental) and S (social) factors in 'Social Responsibility Analysis' on page 215.

However, in my view the G in ESG should come first. The governance factor shapes companies' approaches to E and S, as well as the way that they prioritise development in a world of constant change. In other words, a company's corporate governance is important to investors since it reveals business integrity and direction.

To examine governance, use the checklists for Board Leadership, Ownership Strength, Executive Compensation and Capital Allocation as these are all crucial components of good corporate governance. The average score for these four supporting sub-categories provides a good proxy for governance quality and can help measure the extent to which a board is likely to promote the interests of all shareholders. After all, companies are run by human beings. Poorly structured incentives, weak oversight and limited checks on power are very likely to lead to poor decision-making at best and something far less pleasant at worst.

# BUSINESS PASSION ANALYSIS

IS THE CEO PASSIONATE ABOUT
THE BUSINESS OPPORTUNITY?

The hallmark of all truly great business leaders and entrepreneurs is that the business is their life and career, not just a job. Conversely, if you can identify them, you should avoid the 'tourist manager' who is just in it for the glory, passing through on the way to something bigger.

When Warren Buffett was once asked how he determines which managers to partner with, he said "the biggest question I ask myself is 'Do they love the money, or do they love the business?'" and "Passion is the number one thing I look for in a manager."

Often, it's the leadership's vision and passion that ignites the business opportunity. Both qualities that must be combined with tenacity, which is a necessary ingredient for success because rewards are often far off in the future. That's why a large compensation package will never be as powerful as internal motivation, like following our interests and end up doing what we love for work.

In the end, most companies end up making money from something other than their original idea. The idea is nothing, whereas passion and tenacity are everything. There has to be an energising force. Business biographies tend to show precisely this – how passionate people who live and breathe their business created something out of nothing.

That's why the ultimate question is; "Is this person going to dedicate his or her life to make something extraordinary happen?".

Companies like Alibaba, Amazon, Google, IKEA, Spotify and many others have or had founders who focus relentlessly on pleasing their customers and thinking about strategies that will impact their companies' values 10 or 20 years down the road. Such founders have not just 'skin in the game', but 'heart and soul in the game'.

## BUSINESS PASSION CHECKLIST

1. Does the CEO have a visionary attitude towards the business's opportunities?
2. Does the CEO think independently and exhibit original ideas?
3. Does the CEO have strong market insight?
4. Has the CEO stayed in the same industry for more than a decade?
5. Does the CEO show genuine excitement for their products?
6. *Does the CEO serve on a significant number of outside boards?*

∽

### 1. Does the CEO have a visionary attitude towards the business's opportunities?

*Why does it matter?*

Great management can envision a great future and articulate a cohesive and logical strategy to get there. Such CEOs are rational long-term thinkers who look way ahead and are determined to drive things forward. With a clear vision for the company, they typically invest for the longer term by focusing on what is best for the customer and not just short-term profits. These CEOs act like long-term owners of a business, not like caretakers. In other words, long term here means focusing on customer needs over time – both what will change in them and what will not.

Long-term thinking and adaptability are two sides of the same coin. CEOs who spend significantly more of their time thinking about the long term and have long-term plans generally excel at adapting to change. This focus helps because it makes CEOs more likely to pick up on early signals and make strategic moves to take advantage of it. As evolutionary biologist Charles Darwin said, "It is not the strongest or the most intelligent who will survive but those who can best manage change."

Leaders who can't see it, probably won't find it. CEOs who lack vision cannot inspire teams, motivate performance, or create sustainable value. Poor vision, tunnel vision, vision that is fickle, or a non-existent vision will cause leaders to fail.

*How to assess it?*

Try to assess if the CEO has a vision that they can translate into a strategy to make the company a long-term winner, not just a good story. This kind of CEO is typically progressive and research-minded and can articulate a worldview beyond company operations – one that factors in global social, environmental, and economic issues. There should be a vision based on analysis of future industry trends that will necessitate course corrections from time to time as the competitive landscape change.

A CEO who exhibits a visionary attitude is typically convincing about their vision and how to achieve their objectives. Always ask the CEO how he or she measures success in the company, by what means, where they want to be in the next five to 10 years and how they will get there? What does the CEO consider to be the most important long-term challenge facing the company? What initiatives are being taken today to grow the business further and increase shareholder value?

Be very cautious if the CEO struggles to articulate a vision of where he or she sees the company in the next five to 10 years. Likewise, shun CEOs with an improbable (weak) long-term vision for the future. Without a strong vision, a company is wandering directionless.

If the CEO is a rational long-term thinker with a clear vision for the company, the stock is scored one point.

## 2. Does the CEO think independently and exhibit original ideas?

*Why does it matter?*

Not thinking independently leads to mediocrity. Building a great company is about figuring out what competitors have missed and finding a solution. In other words, a good company will change in line with competitors, but a great company will lead the way as it moves past 'best practices' in search of 'next practices'.

A CEO who has demonstrated the ability to think independently has a sound plan for the business. A plan that is not about copying the past success of competitors, but rather about meeting the customers' needs and wants or how the company could become a better version of itself.

*How to assess it?*

Look for CEOs who question the status quo and engage with bold new ideas and initiatives. This approach involves finding new pockets of value in the industry and being creative over time. Such CEOs typically don't benchmark against their competitors, but rather march to their own rules by focusing on what customers really want and need and bringing a better product to market. A good example of creativity could be a strategy that adapts a proven business model or idea from another market for their own market.

These CEOs are often founders and corporate outsiders who bring fresh approaches and perspectives thanks to not being weighed down by the traditional industry rules. In turn, this should lead them to maintain some distance from conventional wisdom, where companies imitate one another in destructive group thinking by assuming competitors know something they don't. This is the consistency and commitment bias Charlie Munger talked about in his great speech 'The Psychology of Human Misjudgement'.

Always be very cautious towards CEOs who are unable to see past the current paradigm and the way things have always been done. This type of leader is typically obsessed with what others are doing and is likely to seek to replicate the success of a competitor's breakthrough products or profitable business lines. This is the surest path to mediocrity.

If the CEO challenges conventional practices and remains unaffected by what competitors are doing, the stock is scored one point.

## 3. Does the CEO have a strong market insight?

*Why does it matter?*

CEOs need to have deep market awareness and a strong sense of future market needs to ensure long-term growth. With poor market perception, the result is usually valueless research and development.

Ask the CEOs of these companies detailed questions about what is going on in a certain market or region and they know the answers. This is critical for developing the company's strategy, to put more distance between it and the competition.

*How to assess it?*

The CEO should be able to clearly explain the state of the industry and how they are taking advantage of current trends, what they are doing uniquely, why this approach will succeed, and show some numbers to back up their claims.

The details in their answer to the following questions will make it clear whether the CEO has a solid understanding of their customer base, market and competition: "What trends are shaping your industry?"; "What causes companies in your industry to fail?"; "What does your company do that your competitors can't?"; and "How do you convert that into an estimate of future cash flows?"

Be wary if the CEO denies that the company has competition or insists that it does not take its competitors seriously. When a CEO claims their company to have no competition, it's typically because he or she is clueless about their target market or there isn't a need for their product. Even if it is substitutes or alternatives, or other things competing for wallet share or a customer's time, every company has some competition.

If the CEO has deep industry knowledge and a solid understanding of their market, the stock is scored one point.

## 4. Has the CEO stayed in the same industry for more than a decade?

*Why does it matter?*

A manager who has remained in the same industry for an uncommonly long period of time is likely to pursue his or her passion and is likely to have developed talent. A major part of success can be boiled down to doing one thing consistently for an uncommonly long period of time. A beneficial side effect of this is that this type of manager typically develops deep industry knowledge and expertise in building the necessary technology or service and has a vast personal talent network to recruit from. Ideally, they are the company founder or a long-tenured manager who has spent their whole career at the company.

However, industry veterans often get accustomed to a certain way of doing things or thinking about them and struggles to approach problems from a different perspective – to think independently and exhibit original ideas (this is the check #2 on page 41).

*How to assess it?*

Constructing a chronology of the CEO's career will help to understand their background, how they rose to lead the business.

If the CEO has remained in the same industry for more than a decade, the stock is scored one point.

**5: Does the CEO show genuine excitement for their products?**

*Why does it matter?*

The best managers are product enthusiasts who bring products to market that they would personally buy but cannot find elsewhere. Such managers are passionate about their job and work towards their organizational goals with intensity and genuine excitement. They are determined to succeed and typically have a strong focus on market leadership, by being the first to offer a product or offering the best one.

Creating something new, improved and more beneficial reflects their dissatisfaction with the status quo. Instead they are focused on leading change and innovation to keep their organizations fresh, dynamic and growing. The bottom line is: if they don't love and believe in what they are building, they are likely to give up at some point along the way due to the scepticism and setbacks that every business will inevitably face.

*How to assess it?*

Listen to interviews with management or, better yet, interview them yourself to assess whether a CEO is obsessed with their business and building a great product by focus on customer needs. Does he or she seem enthusiastic about the company and obviously proud of it?

However, beware technology-first managers, as they often develop the product they themselves want and avoid engaging with customers.

Look for signs of deep conviction about the problem they are trying to solve for customers. They understand what customers want and ultimately have personal experience with this problem. Other common traits are a strong belief in problem-solving and implementing solutions, always striving to move faster and be better, as well as exceptional work ethics and obsessive attention to detail.

They are typically not satisfied with simply having a successful company. In the end, they have an unquenchable desire to build a business that will break records with huge amounts of competitive spirit. They just love what they do. Notice the fairly high number of people on the Forbes Richest list who 'were never in it for the money'.

Likewise, these people tend not to be high-profile individuals as their ambition is to grow their companies to greatness, not themselves. They typically put the company's well-being before their own convenience.

Moreover, they are generally more motivated by the day-to-day process than the end-game. As this type of person almost never starts a business with the intention of selling it, they typically don't have an exit strategy.

If it's a pre-revenue company, look for founders and early employees with a track record of success sacrificing an enormous opportunity cost to pursue this start-up because they believe in it. Think about how much the team would earn if each put out their CVs tomorrow.

If the CEO is a product enthusiast with great optimism for solutions, the stock is scored one point.

*6: Does the CEO serve on a significant number of outside boards?*

*Why does it matter?*

The CEO's role is a position of great responsibility and time demands. Sitting on multiple outside boards may threaten his or her ability to attend to the business of their primary employer.

*How to assess it?*

In this question you consider the total number of public board seats held by the CEO (including the company). All subsidiaries with their own publicly-traded stock are counted as individual boards.

Excessive board memberships – more than two outside boards (three in total) raises concerns of governance risk. After all, managers who are truly passionate about their business have less time for other activities, such as sitting on the board of other public companies.

If the CEO serves on more than two outside boards (three in total), this check is flagged.

This factor has a zero-weight impact on the scoring model for People and is included as additional information to assist with investment decision-making.

# EXECUTION CAPABILITY ANALYSIS

## DOES MANAGEMENT APPEAR TO HAVE STRONG EXECUTION CAPABILITIES?

A key characteristic of strong leadership is the ability to execute well. At its core, execution simply means getting things done. Effective execution is a key determinant of business success or failure.

The core of executing a company's strategy is in three processes – the people process, the strategy process, and the operations process. In other words, the quality of execution depends a lot on quality of strategy and managers' ability to link operations to strategic goals and human capacity.

You will take less risk partnering with managers who have a proven track record of running a business because you can give more weight to their history. The challenge with evaluating performance is that it often takes years to see how things play out. But there are a number of tell-tale signs that indicate ability to execute on opportunities. However, do not confuse execution with passion for product and customers, or market insight.

## EXECUTION CAPABILITY CHECKLIST

1. Does management have complementary skills and relevant sector experience?
2. Have the senior team and CEO been together for more than five years?
3. Is there a sound strategy for long-term growth?
4. Does management tend to deliver on promises, on time and according to plan?
5. Has the CEO done it successfully before?
6. *Does the CEO face personal challenges that might cloud his or her judgement?*

**1. Does management have complementary skills and relevant sector experience?**

*Why does it matter?*

It all comes down to whether the senior management team has complementary skills and a long track record of relevant sector experience. If they do, the odds are in your favour – particularly if there is a long learning curve in the sector.

*How to assess it?*

To better understand the likelihood for success, evaluate the quality of each executive and what skills they bring to the team. Make sure management represents a diverse skillset and depth of industrial experience within the sector, ideally with international companies.

Here are some things to look out for when checking up on the management team's professional backgrounds:

a) bios that contain no specific roles or company names for their executives (at least for the past 10 years) typically don't have them for a reason, and it's unlikely to be positive;

b) discrepancies between executive bios on the company's website and those you find for the same people elsewhere;

c) bios that contain no educational references;

d) company websites that have no management/director bios;

e) CEOs and CFOs who have never held these positions before.

If the senior management team has complementary skills and average experience of at least five years in the sector, the stock is scored one point.

## 2. Have the senior team and CEO been together for more than five years?

*Why does it matter?*

A good indicator of a strong management is how long the CEO and the senior management have been serving the company together. Long tenure is a great signal of intrinsic motivation and confidence in the business, as well as a good sign that the management has the ability to work as a team. Ultimately, you want to understand how they've performed in both difficult and favourable business environments as this provides a means of measuring their credibility.

*How to assess it?*

Check whether top managers' median tenure at the company is over five years. Ideally, most have been promoted from within, accumulating experience in multiple positions and refining their understanding of the customer base.

Increased turnover at the top can be a sign of trouble. If top managers are heading for the door, it's not a sign of a management team with a history of success together. It's rather an indication of a business that's deteriorating, or that the company is not able to retain high-quality talent. Also, a CEO who keeps forcing out immediate subordinates is likely spending too much time on internal power struggles and not enough on running the business. This makes it difficult or impossible for the company to build momentum and move fast.

Finally, it helps a lot to do some background work with people the management team have worked with in the past. These should be people who know them well, have seen them in leadership positions and can fairly evaluate if this is a strong team that will drive the business forward.

If the median tenure of the company's top managers is more than five years, the stock is scored one point.

## 3. Is there a sound strategy for long-term growth?

*Why does it matter?*

A good management should set out goals and strategies for the company. A collection of intentional decisions, that will provide a context for all decision making. Accordingly, the quality of a management's execution depends a lot on the quality of their strategy. A well-developed, simple strategy for long-term growth is probably the most important pillar of any business.

Management should clearly state its long-term plan for how the company is supposed to grow and protect the business against competition. The latter is one of the most important tasks for any CEO, to widen the moat of the business.

At the same time, beware leaders who are satisfied with the status quo, or who tend to be more concerned about survival than growth, as they won't do well over the long run. As the saying goes, "standing still is going backwards".

*How to assess it?*

When assessing a strategy's credibility, the goal is to get a general sense of the direction of value and whether it is positive or negative, instead of trying to quantify the magnitude. Focus on management's key assumptions about the customer's present and future demand and how they are going to work closely with them to anticipate and meet their needs. Talk to the company's competitors because they generally will give you a different point of view on the industry and about why some strategies are inferior. That said, it takes time for some business models to demonstrate that their strategy will work. Nonetheless, always look out for warning signs of strategy drift.

It's important to understand the system a business has in place to implement its strategy. A successful strategy must be tailored to what the company says it stands for, how it operates, and its limitations. It should be committed to an identity rather than just focusing on growth. Otherwise the odds are that the strategy won't work. As investing legend Philip Fisher put it: "More successful firms usually have some unique personality traits – some special ways of doing things that are particularly effective for their management team. This is a positive not a negative sign." Accordingly, look for companies that embrace their corporate culture rather than attempting to recreate it when trying something new.

Similarly, favour companies that invest selectively to be different. However, keep in mind that competitiveness is far more about doing what customers value than the company's core competence. Yet picking strategic outcomes that are supposed to bring value to the customer is exactly where many companies fall short. Always ask what the most important factors are in winning customers to understand how the company is trying to differentiate itself. Is it price, quality or customer service?

A questionable strategy is one that is difficult to understand or seems to have no prospect of creating value, neither creating defensibility nor connecting to the company's culture and limitations. The weaker the fit between culture and strategy, the worse the performance. However, strategy can be undermined by operational failure, by a misguided view of competition, and, especially, by moves to make the company bigger, rather than better.

Finally, always ask how management proposes to achieve its profit margins. Many small companies manage some initial success but are unable to repeat it year after year. Be sceptical of claims about getting superior returns from doing the same old things better or generating good margins quickly from poor companies. The latter is particularly rare, except when emerging from a broad recession.

Ideally, management's plans will deliver growing volume and earnings over the next five years at least. Moreover, a well-defined strategy statement should include the following information:

1. Description of how the company intends to meet or exceed the needs and wants of its customers;
2. Description of how the company intends to differentiate a business from the competition;
3. Prioritisation of opportunities to grow the business and actions that support growth;
4. Disclosure on competitive moats (if any) and how the company will gain or widen these to insulate against competition over the long term;
5. Performance milestones that are set to capture the underlying strategy and determine success;
6. Link between strategy and capital discipline to ensure a sound financial position.

If there is a well-defined and credible strategy for long-term growth, the stock is scored one point.

For more on how a strategy should be crafted for long-term growth, see 'Proxy Guide: Corporate Strategy' on page 61.

## 4. Does management tend to deliver on promises, on time and according to plan?

*Why does it matter?*

Management teams that are good at executing tend to be less 'accident'-prone and tend to deliver on their promises. It is one thing to consistently earn impressive profits, but to make commitments and deliver shows both management's confidence in the business, and also the visibility of its future earnings. Also, timely execution is usually embedded in a corporate culture where diligence is stimulated and rewarded.

*How to assess it?*

The question to ask is, has management met the objectives mentioned a few years ago, assuming the same CEO is still in place? Not just 'talk the talk' but 'walk the talk' as action always speaks louder than words. Here, any inconsistencies in management's communication and action should be considered a yellow flag as it will undermine investors' faith in management and the company. However, be wary of recency bias when you evaluate the track record.

Look up prior investor presentations to see how well they did with earlier promises – history often repeats itself. For example, have the proceeds of previous issues not been used as promised, or new plans not executed once announced or even never realised? Managements with good execution skills do not issue frequent profit warnings and downward adjustments of long-term financial targets or announce recently discovered kinks in an acquisition made two years earlier.

If management tends to deliver on their promises, on time and according to plan, the stock is scored one point.

## 5. Has the CEO done it successfully before?

*Why does it matter?*

A good CEO will have a solid CV with a history of exemplary performance. While past performance is not always a certain indicator of future events, a long-term track record of success should not be taken lightly. Someone who has consistently experienced success in leadership roles has a much better chance of success than someone who has not.

The bottom line is that unproven leaders come with a high risk premium. Smart companies and investors recognize potential, but they reward performance. Moreover, for managers who have been successful before it's more about legacy and the fun they have, as these factors are typically not driven by financial considerations.

*How to assess it?*

It's all about having early evidence of product/market fit. Look for a manager with a history of creating long-term value for shareholders, whether at the current company or in the same industry.

Long-term value often manifests itself in the trend of market share. If the CEO has proved that they can create a market or gain share (or did so in prior roles), it will reduce the likelihood of mistakes. Likewise, it is always worth trying to check the EPS growth record of the CEO's previous company.

If it's a pre-revenue company, look for traction. Traction can be active users, pre-sales, beta testers, letters of intent, etc. Think about the traction Twitter generated for five years before beginning to monetize.

Ideally you want a manager who has deep knowledge of the business, as there are few cases where outside managers tend to be good hires. The best type of outside managers are those who don't make changes quickly and try to understand the business and its customer base.

A good trait for outside managers is if they solicit the opinions of employees before they implement major changes. If instead they start to make changes immediately after joining the business, it is likely that he or she will fail.

Lastly, formal announcements of the retirement of CEOs should not be taken too seriously. Sometimes they are completely genuine, but on other occasions they can be a polite way of saying he or she is incompetent.

If the CEO has done it successfully before, the stock is scored one point.

### 6. Does the CEO face personal challenges that might cloud his or her judgement?

*Why does it matter?*

This check offers an assessment of whether the chief executive is going through a tough time personally that might cloud his or her judgement. The bottom line is that what goes on in the personal lives of CEOs can matter to the company.

The fact that negative life events like illness, bereavements, divorce, alcohol/drug abuse or financial problems often have a negative impact on the business, due to their stress and emotional pain, should be of great interest to investors. Think about the impact on focus, on behaviour, and on the CEO's attitude towards risk. A distracted CEO could harm long-term decision-making and cause the company to miss out on potential opportunities.

For example, in a divorce the CEO may not have the cognitive capacity to focus. Their energy may be sapped. They may also be at risk of losing a large portion of their wealth. If so, the incentive plan may go out the courthouse window. It's not uncommon for divorced CEOs to resign for one reason or another within a year or two of their divorce.

*How to assess it?*

The difficulty for investors who might want to understand this risk is that their interest in this kind of information runs directly counter to the CEO's right to personal privacy. However, following the news will probably do the work for you as these kinds of development tend to leak out.

Another way to getting a sense of what's going on with the CEO's primary non-work interests like family, health and hobbies is to track social media platforms. These can be a great way of gaining insight into somebody's areas of interest outside work.

Still, CEOs are seldom active on social media platforms. Accordingly, you might have to do some channel checks too. See 'How to Conduct Your Channel Checks' on page 349.

Arguably, the CEO's personal problems ought to trigger disclosure when they have clear and direct impact on company performance. Yet most companies do not disclose them. Even when they do, the reports often only come out later – for example, when the CEO sells shares to satisfy the terms of a divorce settlement or when health concerns over the CEO prove fatal after the company has covered up their illness and downplayed its seriousness for as long as possible.

If the CEO has personal challenges that might cloud their judgement, this check is flagged.

This factor has a zero-weight impact on the scoring model for People and is included as additional information to assist with investment decision-making.

# PROXY GUIDE: CORPORATE STRATEGY

A sound strategy is about being different by doing something important for the customer that is not easily replicable by competitors – namely an antidote to competition. In other words, companies need products that are unique or offered in a distinctive way to justify high profit margins, but also defensibility to protect those high profits. In other words, in businesses with no sustainable competitive advantages, new inventions help customers save money. In businesses with sustainable competitive advantages, new inventions help the bottom-line (and the owners by extension).

For more on defensibility through sustainable competitive advantages, also called moats, please read the 'Proxy Guide: Competitive Moats' on page 199.

Strategy is the series of choices made about where to play and how to win to maximize long-term value. It's as much about choosing what to do as it is choosing what not to do. There are basically two choices when it comes to strategies:

1. Aim to dominate the entire industry or, target a market segment in which the company can excel (e.g., regional and/or niche market);
2. Offer bargain prices or the best customer relationship or win by marketing superior products (see 'Differentiation Strategy' below).

Evaluating a management team's strategy in the context of these choices will give an idea of the company's future performance. Keep in mind that a corporate strategy should be simply explained, not overloaded with unnecessary information. The latter can reveal leaders lacking in strategic confidence.

Yet, strategy is typically something that evolves over time as smart managers are responsive to their markets and as their customers develop. It is essentially the idea that a company can craft the conditions to create durable returns for its shareholders to get long periods of outsized returns. However, as Richard Rumelt explains in his great book *Good Strategy Bad Strategy*: "Fortunately, a leader does not need to get it totally right – the organisation's strategy merely has to be more right than those of its rivals." Successful strategies often owe as much to the inertia of competitors as to the strategy itself.

Generally speaking, the most successful growth companies are more specialised, have stronger differentiators and pursue a narrower customer base than their more average peers.

For example, when a business tries to appeal strictly to a niche market rather than the masses, it will typically benefit in a number of ways: premium prices, lower costs of acquiring customers, and the opportunity to become the brand that consumers associate with the offering itself. This partly happens because it provides more value to customers than other players through greater knowledge and expertise about the niche. That's why the quality of a business is determined in a broad sense by the quality of its customers.

## DIFFERENTIATION STRATEGY

There are basically three ways to differentiate a business from the competition – superior product, outstanding customer relationship, or lowest cost. Customers know how to identify these types of value and generally don't expect to get them all from a single supplier. Market leaders typically create a true difference in one value discipline while remaining competitive in the two others. Moreover, customers are generally more loyal to companies with superior product or best relationship than to those with lowest prices, so quality is the better way to go if the company has a choice.

**Product leadership**

This involves putting technology to new uses, inventing new products, or focusing on user-friendliness by best-in-class R&D. The latter ensures that the pace of innovation is high (relative to competitors), which creates a virtuous cycle of the strong getting stronger. Rational (but genuine) innovation makes all the difference as long as the company stays one step ahead of the competition as they attempt to copy its success. This includes actual physical and perceived differences, like a unique feature or reputation of being superior.

Common Moat Sources: Network Effects, Special Assets and Brand Loyalty.

**Customer closeness**

This involves focusing on the customer more than anything else by being responsive to their pain points, needs, and desires in order to deliver the 'best total solution'. Some make this a true benefit, to best serve customer needs and offer convenience and efficiency. Success depends on a niche market focus and strong sales force with appropriate targeting, efficient management of customer relationships, and tailored offers. This is particularly valuable for complex products where the salesperson acts as an advisor, as it typically includes all supporting elements such as training, installation and easy ordering. However, it is trickier to maintain customer intimacy at scale.

Common Moat Sources: Switching Costs and Brand Loyalty.

**Low-cost provider**

Products positioned in line with the market average, at the best price, with a minimum of hassle (i.e., reliable product or speedy service). The low-cost provider's product range is simple above all as costs are slashed by cutting out elements that don't address the needs of the majority. Moreover, cost leadership is critical to success, something that comes from having large scale and operational excellence.

Common Moat Sources: Scale Economies and Process Power.

Finally, operational excellence is a prerequisite to succeeding with any differentiation strategy over time, but does not by itself assure differential margins. That is to say, operational excellence is not a strategy in itself as competitors can often easily imitate the improvements yielded by it, eventually arbitraging out the value to the business. Pursuing operational excellence is simply an ongoing process of improvement to become better at the things that make the business profitable and valuable today.

The bottom line is that companies should try to be unique instead of trying to be the best at something. In other words, when it comes to strategy, focus should be on invention and then building competitive moats around it. The first cause of a strategy is always invention.

Innovation means reacting to trends or shifts much faster than competitors in order to stay different. It's about reacting to significant structural changes in the industry's economics or customer behaviour. It involves taking advantage of new technologies, business models or using existing ideas in a new way, whether as an early-stage company or a mature company considering a new direction.

Nonetheless, there are also rare times when no new opportunities have developed and no new risks have appeared. Here doing more of the same may be the most reasonable strategy.

## GROWTH STRATEGY

For CEOs to win the support of their board and investors, they need the ability to develop and explain how their strategy can scale up – not just how they will differentiate their business to survive. In this sense the goal for growth should be for the largest number of customers possible to enjoy the product on offer without diluting its competitive advantages.

Still, the objective of sound growth is not only to make gains, but to build defensibility through sustainable competitive advantages. Without the latter, high returns cannot be protected over time and growth will create little or no value. It will merely be a commodity business, because as soon as the growth in demand slows down, the profits will vanish. In other words, a competitive advantage that isn't sustainable will merely be an opportunistic window of time for the business.

For example, strategies that focus on market share alone typically come at a high cost as they often erode profit margins and competitive advantages while their offerings become commoditized. High levels of capital spending and rapid increases in market share, often as result of deal mania, are tell-tale signs of a management racing out of control.

All the same, companies pursuing high growth tend to follow three well known strategies:

(1) Serving broader stakeholder needs;

(2) Creating new markets;

(3) Changing the rules of the game.

The best opportunities for growth are those that are focused on core or related markets (complementary products for example) where the company's existing competitive moats may give it a defence against competition. The next-best growth opportunities come from entering virgin markets with no dominant player enjoying sustainable competitive advantages, to fulfil a yet unmet demand. This avoids price wars from head-on competition with established players as it's incredibly difficult to replicate all of industry leaders' natural advantages – from brand loyalty to customers and assets. The third best growth opportunity comes from changing the game entirely in an established market through disruption. The latter two are key when a company's growth potential is limited within its core markets.

To succeed in changing the rules of the game it naturally takes a counter-positioning strategy that involves innovation of a new, superior business model that established competitors does not adopt due to anticipated cannibalisation of their existing business. This business model, by itself, constitutes a competitive moat – a special asset. Nonetheless, a counter-positioning strategy tends to first target lower-end customers or lower-feature products with a seemingly inferior product and then evolve to be good enough for high-end users. Also, a successful counter-positioning strategy typically involves a different organisation with different people, world view and compensation structures compared to the established competitors.

The idea of a counter-positioning strategy is discussed in detail by Hamilton Helmer in his remarkable book *7 Powers: The Foundations of Business Strategy*, which I recommend highly.

# CAPITAL ALLOCATION ANALYSIS

DOES MANAGEMENT APPEAR TO USE SHAREHOLDERS MONEY WELL?

One of management's most important jobs is to allocate capital with the objective of building long-term value per share. Successful capital allocation means converting inputs, including money, things, ideas, and people, into something more valuable than they would be otherwise. Simply put, capital allocation is the link between business value and shareholder value.

One benefit of investing in a management team with great capital allocation skill is that you can thrive in market downturns. Value creation in these companies can come from share repurchases or organic growth in market share or compelling acquisitions.

Basically, CEOs have five choices for deploying capital – investing in existing operations, acquiring other businesses, paying dividends, paying down debt, or repurchasing stock – and three alternatives for raising it – tapping internal cash flow, issuing debt, or raising equity.

The best way of assessing managers' skill in capital allocation is to review whether their decisions have improved earnings per share over time. If the chairman and CEO are long tenured, it's easier to imagine that future capital allocation will be similar to past capital allocation. If a CEO has been running a company for decades, a look at the long-term stock chart should suffice.

The best CEOs tend to be the ones who regard capital allocation as their most important task. Yet, most companies pay little attention to it due to inexperience in capital markets and corporate finance. Most CEOs get the top job because of operational excellence, corporate politics or other skills that have nothing to do with allocating capital. Also, many boards are similarly inexperienced when it comes to capital allocation.

## CAPITAL ALLOCATION CHECKLIST

1. Do the company's incentive plans encourage long-term value creation?
2. Do investments and acquisitions focus on strengthening the core business?
3. Is there consistency in the people responsible for capital allocation?
4. Has the company taken opportunistic action over an attractively priced stock?
5. Have total shares in issue remained constant or decreased over time?
6. *Does the company lack a sound dividend payout policy?*

### 1. Do the company's incentive plans encourage long-term value creation?

*Why does it matter?*

This check offers an assessment of whether the incentives a company has in place encourage judicious capital allocation. Incentives matter when managers choose between optimising the appearance of accounting and maximising the present value of future cash flows. Managers who are paid handsomely to misallocate capital will do so.

The objective of capital allocation is to build long-term value per share in the belief that investors will ultimately follow value. If the market fails to reflect it, management can take action by sharpening communication or buying back stock.

Incentive programs frequently encourage behaviour that is not in the best interest of long-term shareholders. Misaligned incentives tend to manifest themselves in bad decision-making and value destruction. Large bonuses and stock options have been held responsible for overly risky behaviour and short-term strategies.

For example, if remuneration is roughly correlated with the size of the company, management may do value-destroying M&A deals to grow. This could lead to a debt-fuelled buying spree, leaving a hole in the company's balance sheet. As Howard Marks advocates, we must be sure to give adequate attention to second-order effects.

*How to assess it?*

In order for an incentive plan to reward long-term performance, it must tie compensation to results over a time period of at least five years. Where there are mitigating factors that would justify a shorter performance period, these need to be carefully explained to shareholders.

Given that the average CEO stays barely five years in the role, there is typically a mismatch between their aims and those of shareholders. That is why long-term schemes of at least five years that move beyond tenure period are preferable. These do not incentivise inappropriate risk-taking or create adverse, unintended long-term consequences.

A good complementary sign is a significant length of deferral of variable pay. This should apply not just to annual bonuses, but also long-term incentive plans. Companies should explain any mitigating factors that may justify not deferring variable pay.

Equally, they should minimise 'cliff-edge' vesting. Sliding scales starting from suitably low levels of initial payment are preferable.

Significant incentive awards should only be made for exceptional performance where strong performers are differentiated from average performers. Performance targets should be sufficiently challenging so that senior managers rarely receive

100% of their potential bonus entitlement, unless they have been truly exceptional. Likewise, a good rule of thumb is for 50% of the incentives to be based on profits and 50% on underlying business targets reflecting strategic objectives.

If management focuses on delivering strong cash flows and re-allocating capital sensibly, the share price typically looks after itself. Accordingly, the ideal compensation structures are those that reward long-term value creation. That's why the ultimate incentive plans are those that replace long-term incentive pay with a requirement that executives own a multiple of their annual salary in company stock (or pay bonuses in the form of restricted stock) and hold it for long periods of time. For more on ownership, please read question number two 'Does the management team own a significant stake in the business?' on page 119.

In cases where management lacks sufficient 'skin in the game' you should look for good value creation factors or business targets. These should focus on operational drivers (key performance indicators) like cost control, customer satisfaction, and return on capital – the metrics which dictate the business's success or failure. Such indirect incentives should stop managers from focusing too much on short term share price movements.

According to Warren Buffett, a good incentive plan "should be (1) tailored to the economics of the specific operating business; (2) simple in character so that the degree to which they are being realized can be easily measured; and (3) directly related to the daily activities of the plan participants."

Success measures like market share, accounting income, sales, absolute growth and EBITDA are all considered to be poor proxies for value creation. For example, an excessive focus on sales growth could result in a willingness to sacrifice margins to generate incremental growth 'at any cost'. Likewise, if expansion of market share is the only thing that matters, it is easy to sacrifice profitability or cash flow along the way to achieve that end.

Examples of poor incentives are option awards or other traditional bonus structures that provide managers with upside rewards without downside risks in the event of poor performance. Other bad signs to look for are a lack of incentive plans, no disclosure, absence of financial targets, and the lack of a long-term plan. Likewise, beware any retesting of performance conditions for incentive plans.

If incentives are primarily tied to long-term value creation factors over a time period of at least five years (or less if mitigating factors justify this), the stock is scored one point. Likewise, if management as a group owns 5% or more of equity or a majority of senior managers have a significant portion of their net worth in the company (shares with a value of five times or more their base salary, for example), the stock is also scored one point.

Unvested shares in incentive arrangements should not count towards the total.

## 2. Do investments and acquisitions focus on strengthening the core business?

*Why does it matter?*

Successful companies typically stick with what they know best and strengthen their core businesses and competitive advantages rather than engage in conglomerate building. Such companies only acquire companies that are closely related and can offer clear synergies. These bolt-on acquisitions generally have higher success rates than bigger transformational M&A transactions. Put simply, these companies try to stick to what they are good at.

Because management is under pressure to grow and put the best spin on their uniqueness to exploit opportunities, it is not uncommon for investors to be led into over-optimistic conclusions about the prospects of new investments. For most declining businesses, management tends to redeploy cash flow into things outside of their core competencies, to 'diversify' as a desperate attempt in the pursuit of growth. Such compromises and inconsistencies will erode a company's distinct positioning by becoming all things to all customers.

The bottom line is that investing for low returns, either through acquisitions or expanding into lower return areas, can undermine the overall quality of the business. The erosion of longer-term returns for the sake of short-term profit gains will eventually lead to the permanent destruction of shareholder wealth.

*How to assess it?*

Make sure that the company is reinvesting enough (keeping R&D up) at a proven rate of return to stay competitive. Equally, though, be vigilant that any investment and acquisition strengthens the competitive advantage of the core business or fills a strategic gap. The latter could be access to new territories, product segments or technologies or help to achieve growth or critical mass by way of increasing market share.

Always be very cautious towards management teams that are more concerned with growing bigger than using acquisitions to create more value for the company and its shareholders. Sometimes business transformation is necessary because the underlying market is changing in a way which is both rapid and unforeseen. Yet, in most cases risky transformational projects can be avoided if management is visionary and keeps the company evolving towards where it needs to be in five to 10 years.

In contrast, serial acquirers (also known as M&A compounders), do rather small and often private deals rather than 'transformative' public deals. Acquisitions of small private companies tend to be priced more favourably than public companies and generate much better returns – especially when the deals are done through direct contact with sellers to avoid auctions. Small acquisitions also imply lower risk for the buyer. In addition, it's reasonable to assume that multiple acquisitions also build capabilities. For serial acquirers, acquisitions are a systematic process at the core of the strategy.

For any acquisition to succeed it's critical that management understands the business they are acquiring intimately. This explains why vertical deals are seldom successful. For this reason, it is particularly worrying if the acquired company serves different customers or doesn't fit into the core competency of the business. And even more so if the customers and employees don't remain with the acquired business. As Warren Buffett once said, "look for management teams that stick with what they understand and let their abilities, not their egos, determine what they attempt."

A business in flat or slightly declining markets will usually serve shareholders best by focusing on retaining (and maybe growing) their dominant position within their niche, generating as much cash as possible and returning any excess that their strategy does not require to owners through dividends and buybacks. Yet maturing companies usually continue to invest despite declining returns on invested capital. Look at the Cash Flow statement for evidence of M&A.

Another testament to people who make good decisions is what they do when things don't work out as planned. A real tick in the box in favour of the management being a good capital allocator, would be if they can create shareholder value even though an investment or acquisition isn't panning out as hoped.

Divestments (spin-offs) of small non-core businesses are another way for companies to strengthen their core businesses. Yet for most managers it's an unnatural act to shrink their prestige and span of control by spinning off and selling businesses. By the time it becomes clear to them that divestment is the best course of action, shareholders have often been asking for it for years.

If investments and acquisitions have tended to strengthen the company's competitive advantages and core business, the stock is scored one point.

### 3. Is there consistency in the people responsible for capital allocation?

*Why does it matter?*

This check offers a prediction as to whether future capital allocation at the company will be similar to past capital allocation. If the chairman, CEO and CFO are long tenured, it's easier to anticipate that future capital allocation will be similar to past capital allocation – or if the person responsible for capital allocation has a connection to the company's founder.

Short-tenured leadership typically lacks deep knowledge about the business, which may result in poor capital allocation decisions. Also, capital allocation takes time and is usually largely the work of the current CEO's predecessor.

*How to assess it?*

The key question to ask is 'Who is responsible for capital allocation?'

For a very young company that is less than 10 years old, the answer is always short-tenured executives. In this case look for the presence of a founder or controlling family to influence capital allocation. It could also be a former top lieutenant of the founder or a 'refounder' who influences the capital allocation. The latter is someone who has reshaped the business through some sort of crisis.

It's true, though, that over time most companies drift away from the control of the founder, or the founder's family, as more and more outside executives are hired who haven't spent their whole careers at the company. In this case look for a long-tenured chairman, CEO or CFO as the capital allocator. Also, make sure that the person responsible for capital allocation has long experience in capital markets.

If the chairman, CEO and CFO's median tenure and experience with capital markets is over five years, the stock is scored one point. Likewise, if the person responsible for capital allocation has a connection to the company's founder and more than five years of experience with capital markets, the stock is also scored one point.

## 4. Has the company taken opportunistic action over an attractively priced stock?

*Why does it matter?*

This check offers a gauge of management's capital allocating skill by assessing if they have created value by acting on attractive valuations. It includes a history of raising capital opportunistically, repurchasing stock at low valuations, and using a high-priced stock as a currency to make acquisitions.

This typically means that the company is exhibiting counter-cyclical behaviour and patience by accumulating cash to be able to strike when things are cheap. In other words, it looks to invest when competitors are not and vice versa.

Acting opportunistically and not overpaying for things implies that management has a clear sense of what their assets are worth and is willing to act on that knowledge. Whether that means buying or selling, the difference between value and price should always guide management decisions.

*How to assess it?*

The bottom line is that competent capital allocators usually take on more debt and deploy additional cash (instead of hoarding it) during a recession when good opportunities arise. They are typically opportunistic in taking advantage of a high or low-priced stock in three ways:

**Fundraising:** In fundraising, share dilution is probably the biggest risk to investors. That's why it's so important to raise capital opportunistically when one can, rather than when one must, to minimise the dilution in earnings per share. Be on the lookout for CEOs who seem to regularly undertake financings that are more dilutive than similarly situated peer companies.

Watch out for badly structured financing vehicles, like convertibles, rights issues and warrants that are based on the market price at the time of conversion or exercise. Such structures tend to be too dilutive and encourage 'pump and dump' behaviour – something that is common among financially distressed companies that have to resort to rescue financing by issuing new shares in a crisis situation.

**Acquisitions**: Market conditions play a significant role in M&A transactions. When an acquirer's shares are considered overvalued, management may prefer to pay for the acquisition through a share exchange. The shares are essentially a form of currency.

However, beware executives who pay 'strategic' prices for acquisitions. Big companies typically acquire start-ups early in their growth to stay at the cutting edge of technology, particularly when the quest for growth pushes them outside their zone of core competence.

In general, acquisitions that create value through improved efficiencies of the merged organisation should not be attributed to capital allocation skill. It is just management-led improvement that typically reflects a cost-conscious culture acquiring a business that hasn't been run efficiently.

**Buybacks**: Because share buybacks decrease the number of shares outstanding, they have the effect of increasing earnings per share. If the stock is undervalued, these repurchases can add materially to the value of the business. Savvy share shrinkers can use substantial buybacks when the stock is cheap to create a 'double dip' for shareholders and turn solid growth into exceptional shareholder returns over a long period of time. Also keep in mind that dividends are taxed on receipt, whereas the tax on the capital gains resulting from share buybacks is deferred until the investor sells.

If the company has a share repurchase program in place, it's good if management communicates a commitment to buy only at a particular price or valuation. Conversely, it's especially concerning when management announces an enticing buyback plan, but never follows through.

However, beware executives using buybacks simply as a means of increasing earnings per share or offsetting dilution from employee stock options with little regard for the price paid. Conversely, if a company announces a share buyback of more than 10% it is considered a positive catalyst. Supply of the company's stock is tightened as shares overhanging the market are mopped up and cancelled by the buying programme.

If the company has acted opportunistically by taking advantage of a high or low-priced stock, the stock is scored one point.

## 5. Have total shares in issue decreased over time or remained constant?

*Why does it matter?*

Companies have a number of ways of financing their operations. The best do it internally via retained earnings and cash flows, which are then reinvested at attractive rates of return to grow the business. The worst do it externally by over-borrowing and/or frequent share issues. This has a dilutive impact on the business, meaning that earnings now have to go around more investors.

Research has long shown that companies that issue new stock tend to underperform the stock market in subsequent years, while those who buy back shares tend to outperform. Increasing shares in issue can mean that the company is not generating enough cash flow to support the growth of the business.

*How to assess it?*

Check whether total shares in issue have either remained constant or decreased over the last three years. The exception is if the company has been able to increase EPS despite increasing total shares outstanding. This means that that capital used from the issue of securities was used to grow the business faster than it otherwise could have. The latter is generally the case for acquisition stories.

If total shares in issue either remain constant or decrease over time, the stock is scored one point.

## 6. Does the company lack a sound dividend payout policy?

*Why does it matter?*

This check offers an assessment of the company's dividend policy. This reflects management's confidence in future earnings growth. Companies with a sound dividend policy have clear dividend policies in place with consistent track records and rational payout ratios relative to others in the industry.

Paying out dividends forces companies to be more stringent on their use of capital as dividends are real cash outlays for companies that can't be restated. Also, once companies start paying dividend, they are reluctant to stop or cut dividends since it can drive the stock price down and reflect poorly on management's abilities. Yet dividends are not normatively good if the business is funded poorly or if there are better uses for the money.

*How to assess it?*

Any company that intends to distribute a portion of its annual earnings should have an announced dividend policy that is outlined in its annual report. Every company should revisit its dividend policy from time to time. Doing so can greatly improve the strategy debate among a company's senior managers.

Below are some quality criteria to consider when evaluating the dividend payout policy:

**Clear**: Dividend policies should always be clear to reduce shareholders' uncertainty. Basically, this involves explaining what share of earnings will be paid out as dividends each year. This is known as the payout ratio.

Having a clear dividend policy is generally good governance. It gives investors a better understanding of the business they are investing in and what to expect.

It is much easier for a fixed income fund manager to manage their portfolio when they know the dividend policy of each company in the portfolio. After all, these funds are also committed to declare a certain amount of dividend for their owners.

**Consistent**: Companies that pay consistent dividends, are generally trying to increase them annually and cutting them very reluctantly. Consistency is key when comparing the numbers over the past few years. Yet dividend growth can be more difficult for companies with a high payout ratio unless earnings growth is strong.

Investors don't like surprises. A special dividend, while nice in the moment, creates confusion for long-term investors. This is typically the result of a dividend policy not being in place, with payouts being instead set by the board in an ad hoc way and approved by the annual general meeting. This will confuse owners and drive away would-be investors as it makes them less likely to stick to a strategy with dividend-paying stocks.

**Rational**: Several considerations go into interpreting if the payout ratio is rational, most importantly the company's level of maturity. A growth-oriented company that aims to expand, develop new products, and move into new markets would be expected to reinvest most or all of its earnings and could be forgiven for having a low or even zero payout ratio.

If a company can generate high returns on reinvested earnings (>15%) then it should reinvest it, or make value-enhancing acquisitions, or buy back stock at cheap levels, rather than pay its earnings out as dividends. The value of such companies compounds at a much higher rate than if the earnings were paid out to investors as dividends. Even so, dividends are often prioritized by investors and pundits.

In the end, investors should seek to maximise their total return, not yield. The reality is that dividends are the route to average returns. Those who want a dividend can effectively generate dividend-type wealth by selling shares instead. Thomas Phelps said it best in his book *100 to 1 in the Stock Market*: "When you buy a cow to milk don't plan to race her against your neighbour's horse."

Paying out capital through dividends only makes sense if the company lacks great opportunities to put it to work. This can even be considered value-destructive if the payment is effectively financed by debt or equity. The latter is the reason a company with no earnings shouldn't pay dividends. However, when companies with poor capital allocators retain a very high proportion of earnings there is a great tendency for poor investments to be made, which subsequently leads to poor earnings growth and return on equity.

It's fair to expect different payout ratios from different industries. Cyclical and capital-intensive businesses and those with significant value-enhancing investment opportunities should pay out a smaller percentage of earnings compared to companies in defensive industries or those with fewer reinvestment opportunities. The key is to gauge the payout ratio over a business cycle and in relation to industry peers.

A payout ratio above 70% is generally irrational as it might mean the company is failing to reinvest enough of its profits in the business to grow. Also, if business trends unexpectedly fall, there might not be enough profits to keep paying the dividend. A high payout ratio often means the company's earnings are faltering or that it is trying to entice investors who find little else to get excited about.

If the company lacks a dividend payout policy or if the policy is considered unsound, this check is flagged.

This factor has a zero-weight impact on the scoring model for People and is included as additional information to assist with investment decision-making.

# INVESTOR COMMUNICATION ANALYSIS

IS COMMUNICATION WITH SHAREHOLDERS OPEN AND HONEST?

A key factor is the attitude of management towards shareholders. Look for management teams that are candid and honest about the pluses and minuses in their business. You can gain much insight into this by probing shareholder communication. The bottom line is that analysing words is as important as analysing numbers.

The right breed of management teams let the results speak for themselves, and those results should be stated as conservatively as possible. This type of management typically follow the 'under-promise and over-deliver' mantra. Too often, though, senior executives are expected to deliver short-term results, and as a result feel compelled to use unclear language about how they will meet these expectations.

Management teams that tell you too much are almost always the ones that do too little. Such information is rarely true in the first place. Your default response to whatever management tells you about the business should be to validate whether it's true or not. Be sceptical of any statement that management tries to sell to you. Avoid companies that try to present themselves differently than they behave.

Remember that managerial laggards typically sing the same tune, assuring investors that good times are just around the corner. Believing these claims frequently leads to investment mistakes.

## INVESTOR COMMUNICATION CHECKLIST

1. Is management sincere and upfront about the business's difficulties and mistakes?
2. Does the CEO uphold company values and link them to its success?
3. Is management's communication timely and clear?
4. Does management consistently use the same 'story' and key metrics?
5. Is communication focused on long-term business value?
6. *Is management's responsiveness to inquiries poor?*

**1. Is management sincere and upfront about the business's difficulties and mistakes?**

*Why does it matter?*

As a shareholder you have a right to know the challenges and opportunities that face the company. How management communicates mistakes is very important. Being transparent when times are tough goes a long way in building trust and is genuinely appreciated by the investment community.

Great managers communicate both things they have done well and those they have done poorly, in order to paint the most accurate picture possible. Sharing good and bad news with the same degree of regularity and forthrightness enables the company to build its reputation on transparency. In contrast, be cautious towards an over-promotional management team that only emphasizes good news in their communication.

The ability to admit mistakes can be a barometer of overall truthfulness. If a top executive has proven to be less than truthful, there is no telling what other skeletons there are in the corporate closet that have not yet come to light.

*How to assess it?*

Compare three years of shareholder letters in the annual reports and see if they discuss problems openly and how they address them. Ask yourself if the CEO offers a frank report about mistakes that were made and challenges that were met, or do they only mention successes?

Look for managers who openly discuss with investors about their mistakes, what happened and how they plan to get things back on track, rather than simply saying that they had a problem. All the same, you want management to have a healthy dose of paranoia and candour, as they are fully able to recognise and communicate the challenges they face. But they must not have all the answers on difficult strategic issues where the outcome is at best uncertain.

No one is mistake-free, so you should be really concerned about any company where shareholder letters don't discuss problems. This approach tells you that either the team is unable to recognise the problems they face or is unwilling to communicate them. Either undermines management's credibility. The same is true if management make excuses for not communicating with shareholders when confronted with adversity.

Another sign of poor shareholder communication is when mangers offer excuses for weak results and downplay disappointments, rather than addressing the issues. In many of these letters, success is often attributed to management efforts, but failures are attributed to exogenous reasons. If so, this is a sign of a management that avoids its responsibility.

If you start to see statements from companies operating in a similar business and they are increasingly cautious, don't ignore them. Even if your company says things are still fine, it may only be a matter of time before the downtrend reaches them as well. The weakest see it first, but generally a downturn in an industry will catch everyone in the end. When a company forecasts improvements several quarters in the future despite a changing economic environment, it conveys hope rather than facts.

If management is sincere and upfront about the business's difficulties and mistakes, the stock is scored one point.

## 2. Does the CEO uphold company values and link them to its success?

*Why does it matter?*

Almost every company defines a set of company values to underpin the efforts of employees to achieve its goals. Although stating values is common, they can still set a company apart from its competition by clarifying its identity and serving as a behavioral compass for employees.

Clearly defined and shared values directly impact the bottom line, as they create the foundation for day-to-day operational decisions. They guide employees in making moral and practical decisions.

However, what is written in a statement of values is of little importance unless those values are reflected in how the company operates. People act with integrity when their words and actions are aligned – culture lives in the way things get done.

As the industrialist Andrew Carnegie once said, "The older I get, the less I listen to what someone says, and the more I watch what they do." The bottom line is that a company's culture is highly important as it is one of the most stable aspects over time.

*How to assess it?*

Culture always starts at the top. It's the values of the CEO which are transferred down in the company. Values are only incorporated into the culture when employees buy in to them and become accountable for upholding them. That's why the CEO plays a central role in how well employees understand and adopt the company's values, viewing them as a guide to acceptable and unacceptable behaviour. And over time, employees self-select into or out of a culture.

To find meaningful statements of company values you have to look at executive communications and shareholder letters for engaging stories that describe how the company's history and strategies have been shaped by its values. Look for business and leadership principles the company is built upon. To be appropriately described they must be directly linked to a company's success. After all, stories are the foundation of identity and culture lives in the way things get done.

It's a good sign if employees are recognised in shareholder letters as being essential to producing the desired business results as it signals that the CEO is focused on executing its strategy through a strong culture. In all cases you should be very cautious if CEOs spend too much time talking about themselves rather than acknowledging the people they lead.

If the CEO links company values to success in shareholder letters or other executive communications, the stock is scored one point. If unsure, or company values cannot be found as meaningfully described, this check fails by default.

### 3. Is management's communication timely and clear?

*Why does it matter?*

Managers who work to help investors understand their business and its growth prospects are a sign of a shareholder-friendly company. A great management team communicates swiftly and comprehensively, but is also easy to listen to and understand. This is particularly true when they answer questions about important aspects of the business.

When great managers encounter complex concepts, they do their best to educate investors about them by providing discussion of and insight into what they mean. Similarly, they explain clearly to investors how the business is operating and try to make sure market expectations are reasonable in the light of current information. The point is that people trust what they know and understand.

*How to assess it?*

A sign of good shareholder communication is when all get the same level of information promptly at the same time and explained in a way that anyone can understand. If you find it difficult to listen to managers or reading what they write, there's something wrong. You don't want managers employing complicated or non-standard terminology, but rather words and numbers that are easy to understand. When it comes to the financial statements, they should try to guide investors and explain what to look for.

A sign of poor communication with shareholders is when in response to some concern, statements become longer, less specific and more ambiguous. It can seem as if the impact of every word has been weighed, checked and reconsidered before it has been committed to paper. Typically, this means long on detail but short on insight.

In contrast, when all is going well, company statements are clear and concise.

A tip when analysing shareholder letters is to start reading and highlight all clichés such as "employees are our greatest assets", "our future is bright" and "our financial strength." This kind of meaningless jargon and platitudes diminishes anyone's understanding of the business and trust in the leadership.

If you see too much fluff, or more highlighted text than black ink on the pages, it is a warning sign. Whenever it happens you need to ask yourself: does the CEO not understand the business, or does he or she not want the owners to understand it?

After all, you want to understand the business better when you finish the annual report than when you picked it up.

Other warning signs are if management appears to be reluctant to share information about the most important part of the business, as well as deliberate omissions of important facts or statements. Particularly beware management that excludes critics and provides 'selective' access to management.

If management disclose significant matters in a timely and unambiguous manner, the stock is scored one point.

## 4. Does management consistently use the same 'story' and key metrics?

*Why does it matter?*

The 'story' and key benchmarks should be consistent. A lack of consistency in a company's message over time raises concerns about the business's strategic direction. After all, if the company's long-term goals and high-level strategy change every few years, how can anyone have an idea about where the company will be in five or 10 years' time. To put it simply, a business is at great risk when leaders lose their focus.

You should always worry about companies if the script changes. A disciplined and consistent execution of a company's strategy over time is a measure of management's ability, as well as their trustworthiness. Leaders who lack discipline will model the wrong behaviours and will inevitably spread themselves too thin.

*How to assess it?*

Look for consistency, where the executives set out a strategy and stick to it. Regular meetings with management and comparisons of commentary in the annual shareholder letters each year give the opportunity to determine the consistency of the strategic intentions, plans and results. Also, by asking the same questions to management over a period of time you can ascertain if the 'story' remains the same or if it changes.

It's a bad sign if some parts of a strategy are omitted while new priorities are introduced unexpectedly. This is typically a sign of problems ahead.

Watch out for management that cherry-picks performance metrics according to what looks good in the current year – for example, focusing on adjusted operating earnings one year, EBITDA margin the next and the year after that on something else. Also be alive to the risk of mixed messages, with the

CFO communicating a different story than the CEO or the IRO.

If shareholder communication consistently use the same 'story' and key metrics year after year, the stock is scored one point.

## 5. Is communication focused on long-term business value?

*Why does it matter?*

The pressure to increase near-term profits while keeping up with industry peers is certainly one of the major challenges of today's business culture. Warren Buffett once said, "Managers that always promise to make the numbers will at some point be tempted to make up the numbers."

Great management teams focus their communication on long-term business value. Corporate leaders should think in terms of years, not quarters. They communicate their long-term financial objectives and broader operational measures that shape the business´ prospects, and rather gives ranges than point estimates. Long-term financial objectives could be major drivers of income such as volume targets, revenue targets, or major operating costs.

An over-promotional management team is never a good thing as they are managing expectations rather than managing businesses. Ultimately, a hard sell usually indicates that some form of financing is on the way. And when investors eventually discover that the management overstated prospects or made false projections, it becomes very hard for the company to regain its former reputation. Over-promotional managements are also more likely to be involved in frauds.

*How to assess it?*

You can tell by management's actions. Companies with a long-range outlook typically pay attention to cash generation rather than fickle quarterly earnings numbers. They focus on long-term targets and make strategic investments in areas that may only yield results many years down the road.

For example, a management team investing significant resources in delighting customers and improving products is a great sign of a long-term orientation.

A company that is obsessed with quarterly earnings guidance and then comments on whether the targets were beaten or not would definitely give the impression of being focused on the short term. This comes into even greater focus when management talks about the stock price before mentioning the business.

Additionally, read the annual shareholder letters and try to discern whether mangers view shareholders as business partners and co-owners rather than a pesky group they must deal with each quarter. Letters should contain terms like 'intrinsic value', 'return on capital employed', and 'free cash flow per share' rather than simply discussing sales growth.

If management's communication is focused on long-term business value, as opposed to current accounting earnings like short-term guidance, the stock is scored one point.

## 6. Is management's responsiveness to inquiries poor?

*Why does it matter?*

Shareholder-friendly management maintains a responsive dialogue with the investment community. Such mangers are typically happy to provide additional flavour to anyone who is interested. Yet, some management teams seem to be suspicious of the investment community and view journalists, analysts and investors as a necessary evil.

However, the more responsive a company is to issues and concerns, the more credible it will appear.

Management does not need to act on shareholder concerns, but they should at least listen and respond. If management fails to respond to emails, the company will lose investors and alienate analysts – hurting its valuation sooner rather than later.

On the other hand, it makes sense for executives to limit time-consuming interaction with investors and analysts as long as the company provides informative annual reports with detailed business information. If executives focus their time on customers, employees and product they are doing the right thing for investors too. After all, such a prioritisation will have a greater long-term impact on shareholder value and will probably ease investor relations considerably too.

*How to assess it?*

Being responsive means actually responding to questions and concerns, by email or phone. Managers don't need to immediately pick up a ringing phone to be responsive, but they do need to call back. Investors and analysts shouldn't have to wait days or weeks before they hear back to get an answer. A good benchmark response time is 24 hours, but more than a few days is a poor sign.

Do not confuse 'being responsive' with 'appear to be responsive'. The latter refers to the fact that many managers give the appearance of being responsive by addressing current issues and key questions through Q&As, FAQs, webcasts, memos, management interviews, and through company website updates. All of this is clearly positive, but it's not being responsive.

If the company is considered to be unresponsive to questions and concerns, this check is flagged.

This factor has a zero-weight impact on the scoring model for People and is included as additional information to assist with investment decision-making.

# EXECUTIVE COMPENSATION ANALYSIS

DOES THE COMPANY HAVE REASONABLE LEVELS OF EXECUTIVE PAY?

CEO compensation should be examined for abuse. If a material amount of value is being directed to managers at the expense of passive shareholders, and particularly if it does so even in tough times, it's better to look upon them with suspicion.

It is absolutely paramount that management's interests are aligned with those of shareholders. Management-related risks often stem from inadequate alignment of interest between shareholders and corporate executives.

A key to understanding how a management team will probably act is to study how its members are compensated. Appropriate base salary, bonus structure and performance hurdles are required to motivate managers to make prudent decisions that benefit the company and not just themselves.

Examine the company's proxy statement to see the metrics upon which management's variable compensation targets are based, looking for the possibility that such metrics could create adverse, unintended consequences.

## EXECUTIVE COMPENSATION CHECKLIST

1. Does the CEO's pay appear reasonable for a company of this size and profit level?
2. Does the company disclose bonus measures and targets?
3. Does the CEO's pay appear to be in line with other executives?
4. Do the CEO's exit payments appear reasonable?
5. Is the company free of any abuse of options or equity-based incentives?
6. *Does the CEO's pay exceed performance relative to peers?*

**1. Does the CEO's pay appear reasonable for a company of this size and profit level?**

*Why does it matter?*

This check highlights if the CEO's pay appears excessive. Nothing is wrong with paying CEOs well, but to pay them excessively may indicate a lavish corporate governance culture. Highly paid CEOs typically create a money-minded culture in the organisation. Such CEOs usually don't command respect from employees. This presents a risk of damage to the company that will probably be reflected in its earnings sooner or later, as it has implications for customer perception and corporate culture.

Even so, variable pay devices like profit sharing, stock awards, individual bonus plans, and the like are nearly always positive. They're often the mark of a company that truly values its people. They may help to build culture and long-term loyalty and thus foster retention. But too much of a good thing tends to lead to bad behaviour.

*How to assess it?*

To determine whether shareholders are receiving value for money, the CEO's pay is compared to a peer group of at least 12 companies.

The 'pay' mentioned in this question includes only base salary, bonus and non-equity incentive compensation. Perks, pensions and/or equity awards are not considered for this question.

If the CEO's cash compensation ranks outside the 80th percentile among similarly sized companies (by number of employees and profit level), the stock is scored one point.

## 2. Does the company disclose bonus measures and targets?

*Why does it matter?*

We believe that company disclosure is a meaningful signal in its own right. Limited disclosure is often a sign that further investigation is needed – both to rule out poor practice and as a prerequisite to an effective comparison of company performance against peers.

We expect specific targets to be disclosed for past years with sufficient transparency for shareholders to decide if payments have reflected performance fairly. Companies that report only to meet the regulatory disclosure requirements are missing a prime opportunity to engage new and existing investors with the business more fully.

*How to assess it?*

Examine the company's proxy statement and annual reports for the metrics upon which management's variable compensation targets are based.

Some companies justify limited disclosure by the 'commercial sensitivity' of their targets, but this argument has been used too loosely. When commercial sensitivity is cited, you should demand sufficient additional information to be disclosed the following year.

If the company discloses executive bonus measures and targets, the stock is scored one point.

## 3. Does the CEO's pay appear to be in line with other executives?

*Why does it matter?*

The bottom line is that limited difference in compensation among the management team is a good sign. If the CEO makes much more than the other senior executives, this is an issue of corporate governance as it is usually a sign of an all-powerful CEO. Likewise, the pay gap provides insight into the quality of succession planning and management of 'retention risk' – the possibility that executives will jump ship for new posts offering more attractive rewards.

At the same time, note that pay gap often varies with the structure of the executive team (whether there is a COO, for example) and their tenures.

Overall, CEO dominance may indicate long-term problems with the company's compensation practices and, more broadly, its board-level management and oversight. A board that isn't vigilant over executive compensation may not be on top of financial controls either.

*How to assess it?*

Check whether the next highest paid executive's total pay is more than 50% of the CEO's total pay. When considering variable pay elements, include the annualised value of outstanding incentive schemes (share and option plans) upon full allotment, calculated at the current share price.

If the CEO's total pay is less than 200% of the next highest paid executive's total pay, the stock is scored one point.

### 4. Do the CEO's exit payments appear reasonable?

*Why does it matter?*

This check highlights if the CEO benefits from excessive exit payments - a so-called 'golden parachute'. These are lavish severance packages complete with perks for life that are fit for a king, guaranteed pension benefits far outstripping the value of benefits provided to employees, or loans to executives that are eventually forgiven.

All send a clear message to shareholders: we do not respect you as owners, and we do not feel accountable to you as owners. Also, such CEOs typically treat their companies like ATMs.

*How to assess it?*

Examine the footnotes in the company's proxy statement and annual reports for severance (exit) payments. Exit payments upon a change of control that are in excess of 12-month base salary and bonus are considered excessive.

In other cases of termination of their employment it is considered reasonable if the CEO gets a six months' mutual period of notice, or longer period of notice that follows according to law, and the right to 12 months of severance pay on condition that the company is the party giving notice.

Executives should not be entitled to any additional compensation in conjunction with the termination of their employment; no anti-takeover provisions (poison pills), no good-bye perks, no gold-plated pension or lifetime health benefits. Neither should there be an automatic waiving of performance conditions on a change in control situation where you would expect awards to be pro-rated for performance and time.

Ideally, entitlements should be the same as for the rest of the workforce. However, industry practices are currently some way from this ideal and it will take time to transition. Consequently, you should look for differences in pension arrangements for executive directors and the rest of the workforce to be disclosed and justified.

The 'pay' mentioned in this question includes only base salary, perks and bonus. Long-term cash and/or equity awards are not considered for this question.

If exit payments for the CEO don't appear excessive, the stock is scored one point.

## 5. Is the company free of any abuse of options or equity-based incentives?

*Why does it matter?*

Investors need to be aware of dilutive shares, warrants and options as they reduce existing shareholders´ ownership of a company. Such incentive structures aim to replicate the sense of ownership in management, but often fall short. Instead, they only reinforce a short-term focus and incentivise management to keep one eye on their stock option vesting dates – they do not promote long-term sustainable business growth.

The problem is particularly acute when executives hold many more shares through options than they own directly. In this situation, they don't share in the downside as they only stand to profit and will break even in the worst-case scenario. This may make them more prone to take bets with huge upside and downside for the company, and simply hope for the best.

Tech companies typically keep payrolls low by issuing options year after year, which entails major shareholder dilution. However, this strategy also gives the company tax credit on the share issuance, increasing cash flow.

After all, exceptional managers who earn cash bonuses based on the performance of their own business can simply buy the company's shares directly from the open market if they want to, rather than at shareholders' expense.

*How to assess it?*

For option- and stock-based incentives to be considered 'shareholder-friendly', no more than 2% of the company may be transferred to employees annually via options or equity, and transactions should be priced at the full business value – not at a discount. Also, incentive plans need to have an earn-out period of at least 36 months. Anything shorter makes clear that management prioritize itself and its key employees over shareholders.

Restricted stock is always better than options as it exposes the owner to the downside if the stock falls. Moreover, it has to be counted as an expense on the income statement. If stock options are used, they should be priced at full business value.

Non-executive directors should not participate in option or stock-based plans as this puts them at the same level as executives whom they should be monitoring and deciding remuneration for. Likewise, only individuals who can influence the stock price should be paid in equity, which limits the number of eligible executives and key employees.

Individuals with limited responsibility should be rewarded for good work with cash bonuses rather than equities or stock options.

All of the following criteria must be fulfilled for the stock to score one point:

1. Dilution of ≤2% annually via options or equity;
2. earn-out period of ≥36 months per incentive program;
3. options and equity priced at full business value (no discount);
4. CEO must directly own more shares than they are allotted options on;
5. only executive managers and key employees are included in incentive schemes.

If disclosure on option or equity-based incentives is poor or missing, this check fails by default.

## 6. Does the CEO's pay exceed performance relative to peers?

*Why does it matter?*

This check highlights whether the CEO is underperforming in relation to his or her total pay. Shareholder-friendly CEO pay should be aligned with the company's share performance to determine whether shareholders are receiving value for money.

The best way to keep CEO pay in line with performance is to make sure that corporate boards include shareholders with large stakes in the company. Companies that pay bonuses out of total stock return aren't going to issue additional stock if it depresses ROE. They can be counted on to minimize the growth of assets generally and increase owners' equity specifically.

*How to assess it?*

To determine whether shareholders are receiving value for money, a peer group of at least 12 companies is compared on total CEO compensation versus total shareholder return (TSR).

The TSR is measured by the compound annual appreciation in share price over a five-year period (assuming that dividends are reinvested in the stock). The measure is calculated as the difference between the slope of weighted linear regressions for total pay and for total shareholder returns over the period. Performance is considered to exceed pay if the company is positioned below the red line in the chart below. The green line represents the slope of weighted linear regressions for pay and TSR.

**COMPENSATION VS TOTAL SHAREHOLDER RETURN (TSR)**

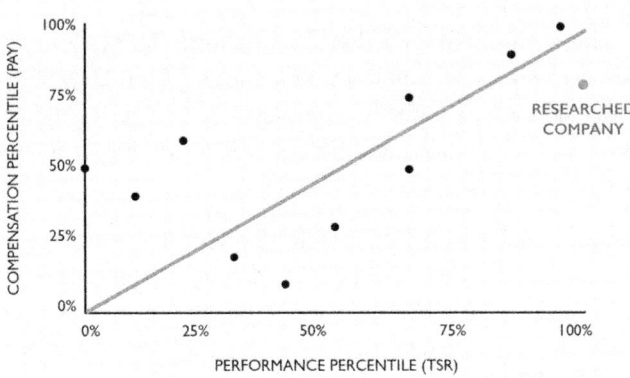

Source: Redeye Equity Research

If the CEO´s cash compensation over the last five years exceeds the TSR in relation to the company's peers, this check is flagged.

This factor has a zero-weight impact on the scoring model for People and is included as additional information to assist with investment decision-making.

NOTE: I am aware of the shortfalls of TSR, but no performance measure is perfect and many are open to manipulation. My view is that TSR is least manipulable over the longer term and will take into account operational performance. Importantly, it is the measure that most aligns company performance with shareholder returns, and this is ultimately how all companies will be measured over longer time horizons. Keep in mind that current performance is the result from efforts made many years ago. This suggests that we might measure the previous CEO's performance rather than the current office holder since nowadays the average tenure of CEOs tends to be shorter than five years.

# PROXY GUIDE: COMPENSATION BASICS

Executive pay disclosure is typically toward the middle of the annual report whereas incentive plans can be found in press releases. Unfortunately, it can be hard to find information regarding compensation in the annual report as the requirements of disclosure are typically simplified for smaller companies.

**Base Salary** is just cash paid regularly during the year, not directly linked to individual or company performance measures.

**Bonus** means variable compensation and includes one-time payouts and/or performance based payouts (*Non-Equity Incentive Compensation*) tied explicitly to a company or individual performance plan. One-time payouts includes hiring, or 'signing-on', bonuses; special awards; severance; and any number of other payouts. These are usually cash payments and can often be deferred. Check the footnotes in the company's annual accounts (not in this book) for specifics.

**Pension** is counted as part of a given year's pay and the amounts the executive will get in the future.

**Equity-based Compensation** are essentially estimates: The true value will fluctuate over time with the company's stock price or other factors. The amounts reported are calculated by more or less uniform methods (according to IFRS2), as of the date that the awards are made to the executive.

- Stock Awards include ordinary shares of company stock, but more commonly restricted stock or restricted stock units, as well as any performance shares, phantom stock or a variety of other similar instruments. They're all alike in that the value is essentially the stock price multiplied by the number of shares or units the executive gets. The ultimate value will fluctuate with the company's stock price.
- Option Awards includes stock options, but also less familiar instruments like stock-appreciation rights. These are all similar in that the ultimate value to the executive depends on the difference between the share price when he or she receives the awards, and the share price when he or she cashes them in (often years later). The value shown in the tables often reflects an estimate or projection, generally calculated with complex but widely used option-valuation formulas.

**Non-equity Incentive Compensation** includes a variety of cash payouts tied to the company's or individual's performance. The most common is the annual incentive bonus, sometimes called defined-contribution benefits, but many companies also have long-term incentive plans based on three or five years of company performance.

**All Other Compensation** is just that: a catch-all for special benefits and perks — from souped-up life insurance and discounted sports tickets to free jet rides or even company-subsidized home renovations.

**Total** is the sum of the other columns, as the name suggests.

Note that pay is reported for the year in which it's earned, so a bonus for performance in 2020 shows up in the 2020 line, even if it will be paid out early in the following year. By contrast, the amounts are calculated at the time of the award; the value of equity-based pay can fluctuate after that point.

# OWNERSHIP STRENGTH ANALYSIS

DOES THE COMPANY HAVE STRONG AND CAPABLE OWNERSHIP?

Companies are much stronger when they have the right shareholders. Ownership structure is a key function for the company development and longevity. If a company has one or more dominant owners, it is usually more important to have a favourable view of those involved than to know everything there is to know about management. Particularly beware companies that flaunt celebrities as partners or investors.

Typically, companies with vague ownership structures have ended up in difficulties that can be traced to weak governance. Such 'ownerless' companies are employee-governed, which allows management to pursue its own agenda without regard to what is best for the company and its owners.

## OWNERSHIP STRENGTH CHECKLIST

1. Does the company have a large outside shareholder on the board?
2. Does the management team own a significant stake in the business?
3. Does the company have a controlling owner with long-term ambitions?
4. Is the founder still involved in the business?
5. Are the principal shareholders' interests aligned with those of minority shareholders?
6. *Does the company have classes of stock with different voting rights?*

**1. Does the company have a large outside shareholder on the board?**

*Why does it matter?*

Quite simply, the risk that management will act in its own interest increases if the owners are absent. The presence of a large non-management shareholder on the board of directors typically means better performance. Such companies are generally better governed, pay their executives more rationally, and the stock typically outperform companies that have no such 'principal' minding the business.

Even if the threat of takeovers and hedge fund activism can have a healthy disciplinary effect on managers, the cost of these efforts is so high that they will always be rare. Most institutional investors simply lack the motivation and the time to effectively discipline or otherwise oversee management.

*How to assess it?*

Examine the shareholder list for large shareholders. A large shareholder is defined for the purpose of this rating as a shareholder that owns 5% or more of a company, while an outside shareholder is a shareholder who is a non-management shareholder. Companies that flaunt celebrities as directors or investors should be approached cautiously.

As a rule, institutional capital prefers to vote with its feet and sell its holdings rather than voice its objections. But institutional owners can be an important complement to principal shareholders and small shareholders when they hold a substantial stake. They can act as a governance watchdog and provide a stamp of approval for the company from the investor perspective. This is an effort that takes place primarily in nominating committees, but also through dialogues with the company alongside the nomination process.

If there is a non-management shareholder on the board of directors with ownership of at least 5%, the stock is scored one point.

## 2. Does the management team own a significant stake in the business?

*Why does it matter?*

Companies are generally more likely to prosper when management has a meaningful ownership stake. A high insider ownership is probably the best protection against fraud. It ensures that they think primarily as owners, not as employees. Typically, a management team with sizable equity ownership retain a long-term perspective for the company, resulting in more prudent operational and capital allocation decisions as they are more likely to explore every alternative before considering a dilutive equity offering. As Nassim Taleb points out in his book *Skin in The Game*; "What matters isn't what a person has or doesn't have; it is what he or she is afraid of losing."

One thing you can generally count on is that managers will behave (despite what they say) in a way that maximises their own wealth. If the stake is too small, ownership becomes more of a symbolic gesture. Then pay and bonuses play a bigger role than their shareholding in how they can personally make or lose money on the company's performance.

Managers that own little or no stock in their company make decisions differently than if they owned a significant stake. This difference may manifest itself in extravagant office furniture, lavish hotels and fancy business cards. It's the difference between careless spending and conservative budgeting. In other words, a management team that doesn't own the business rents the business. They use it how they want and treat capital discipline and shareholders as an afterthought because their own money isn't at stake.

*How to assess it?*

The key is that the managers own enough to care, and to shun those companies in which managers are in a position to 'free-ride' off shareholders without putting any of their own capital at risk. Of course, the bigger the company, the less significant each person's holdings are.

A good complementary sign is if the mangers view frugality as a source of pride. The company headquarters can send the message that each buck counts as it ultimately belongs to the shareholders.

If management as a group owns 5% or more of equity or a majority of senior managers own shares with a value of five times or more their base salary, the stock is scored one point. Unvested shares in incentive arrangements should not count towards the total.

NOTE: While high insider ownership can mean that incentives are aligned to shareholders' benefit, in some situations it may also become a deterrent for institutional shareholder participation, since they will find it difficult to trade large quantities of stock. Also, a limited float makes management immune to potential shareholder action. While a lot of money managers won't invest in such companies due to liquidity issues, it can be your edge.

## 3. Does the company have a controlling owner with long-term commitment?

*Why does it matter?*

This check evaluates if the company is backed by financially strong investors with long-term commitment to the business. Having a cash-rich promoter family or parent company that can and will back long-term initiatives with cash and provide additional capital during periods of stress is a good sign. Moreover, academics have found that stocks of companies with controlling shareholders, including families, outperform those with dispersed ownership.

Controlling owners typically avoid excessive leverage and use retained earnings rather than serial equity offerings to grow. Also, independent thinking is easier in companies with dominant shareholders. These features insulate against pressure from both rivals and stock markets, as they typically focus on long-term value creation.

Ideally, the controlling owners are active with board positions and deep experience in some aspect of the market. Maybe they have worked with these same customers in another context, or they have deep expertise with the technology, or they have built a very similar business in an adjacent market.

*How to assess it?*

Carefully examine the controlling owners' objectives for the company, their finances and their dealings so that you can know as far as possible what lies ahead. A controlling owner is defined for the purpose of this rating as a shareholder or group of shareholders (a family, for example) that controls at least 20% of the company's board seats, with a minimum of two, and has done so for a period of more than three years.

A controlling shareholder at imminent risk of high indebtedness and who may be forced to sell its holdings is not a stable owner. This also applies to owners who lack the financial muscle to back up long-term initiatives with cash when no one else will. In both cases, the ownership structure is at risk of being undermined.

Beware those companies where the major owners don't support growth by not investing in a new issue. A related red flag is if the controlling owners treat the company as a cash cow and don't support sound growth initiatives.

If the company has controlling owners with a long-term commitment to the business, the stock is scored one point.

## 4. Is the founder still involved in the business?

*Why does it matter?*

This check evaluates if the company still has founder influence. We consider it a significant positive for a company if its founder or their family remain significant owners or are still active in the business he or she helped to establish. The founder's 'skin in the game' demonstrates their faith in the business and ensures their interest in the company's long-term success. Also, founder-owned companies generally outperform the market.

Founder ownership creates long-term focus. Companies where the founder still has long-term ownership ambitions typically act generational in their capital allocation perspective. Such companies also tend to be more committed to the development of their employees.

*How to assess it?*

Examine the shareholder list for the presence of a founder. A founder is defined for the purpose of this rating as the person who established the company, but could also be a descendant of the founder(s) or a 'refounder' who has reshaped the business through some sort of crisis. In other words, a founder or an entrepreneur is not always someone who creates a new venture. It is also someone who shifts a business from low to high productivity.

If the (re)founder or their family still owns at least 10% of the outstanding shares and/or is still involved in a managerial position or as chairman of the board, the stock is scored one point.

## 5. Are the principal shareholders' interests aligned with those of minority shareholders?

*Why does it matter?*

Strong owners are not always good for the stock or for other shareholders. One apparent explanation for an owner discount is that the principal shareholder has, or can be suspected of having, interests other than maximising the value of the company, i.e. that power is more important than return. If the principal shareholder considers the company its own, there is a great risk that minority shareholders will be ignored.

You should be extra observant of companies with a second class of stock with super-voting rights, large family or insider ownership, or large government ownership positions. Any of these can have a meaningful impact on executive decisions on capital allocation.

Another obvious case where the principal shareholder's interests diverge from those of other shareholders are companies where the principal shareholder is looking to take over the company entirely.

*How to assess it?*

Ask yourself if the principal shareholders' interests have led to value-destructive decisions. A bad sign is if the company's major or controlling owners have a poor reputation associated with unethical behaviour or profit previously reaped at the expense of minority owners. You will find opinion pieces by searching for phrases like '<Company name> fraud'.

Another example is found in companies dominated by a founding family in which there is reason to suspect that the family retaining control is an end in itself. This is particularly true in cases where family members are perceived as shoe-ins for key positions in the company even though they are not qualified for these jobs. Similarly, a controlling founder may make nepotistic hires of people they are most comfortable working with instead of better qualified candidates.

Short-termism sometimes applies to venture capital companies. Despite their commitment to active ownership, their work with portfolio companies is exit-driven and temporary, with the goal of divesting their investments within the foreseeable future (usually 5-10 years). Uncertainty always ensues when an owner that clearly wants to exit does not have an obvious successor, which often has a negative impact on venture capital-owned companies in the lead-up to an IPO. The same sometimes applies to spin-off companies.

If the company's major shareholders' interests are aligned with those of minority shareholders, the stock is scored one point.

## 6. Does the company have classes of stock with different voting rights?

*Why does it matter?*

The risk here is that the company will focus on keeping insiders happy at the expense of common shareholders. Issuing shares with multiple voting rights allows the founders and management to maintain control over the strategic direction of the company – which increases the risk that management may pursue projects that are not in the best interests of the company, but for their own benefit. In turn, this may imply a higher cost of capital on future fund raising.

Dual-class shares help the founders and management focus on the long-term growth of the company instead of immediate financial return. They can also be seen to be a tool to defend against unwanted takeover attempts, as the controlling parties can vote down takeover proposals by exercising their voting power.

*How to address it?*

Examine the shareholder list for the presence of dual-class shares with different voting rights that confer extra power on insiders.

If the company has dual-class shares with different voting rights, this check is flagged.

This factor has a zero-weight impact on the scoring model for People and is included as additional information to assist with investment decision-making.

# BOARD LEADERSHIP ANALYSIS

## DOES THE BOARD OF DIRECTORS APPEAR TO BE OBJECTIVE AND EFFECTIVE?

The best solution to corporate governance issues is to take great care in identifying CEOs who will perform capably regardless of structural constraints. Outstanding CEOs do not need a lot of coaching from owners, although they can benefit from a similarly high-calibre board, that is well suited to the company and independently minded.

Finding and retain a talented CEO is of outmost importance for directors. But the role of the board is not just to hire, but also to fire the CEO. That's why a sensible analysis of the board focuses on the question: *If it became necessary, would the board have the wherewithal to oppose or even fire the CEO?*

Governance is necessary, but it is not sufficient. Directors must also be chosen for being business savvy, their interest and their ability to represent the owners' interests. In the end, the board's primary function is to advise the management team on achieving sustainable long-term performance. Therefore, directors must assume the role of 'mentor', not 'governor'.

One of the greatest problems among boards is that members are selected for other reasons, such as adding diversity or prominence to a board. Such board members typically view their directorship as a perk, not a responsibility.

## BOARD LEADERSHIP CHECKLIST

1. Is a majority of the board composed of genuinely independent directors?
2. Does the board hold regular meetings without the CEO to review his or her performance?
3. Is the size of the board reasonable?
4. Do most board directors appear business-savvy and shareholder-oriented?
5. Is the company free of abuses of power for personal gain?
6. *Does the chairman serve on an excessive number of outside boards?*

∼

### 1. Is a majority of the board composed of genuinely independent directors?

*Why does it matter?*

The proportion of independent directors on a board is viewed by many as critical to firm performance. This question addresses whether members of the board are subject to control by others. Generally, a board lacking a majority of independent members will raise significant concerns. The largest frauds in corporate history have typically involved board members whose interests were more clearly aligned with management than shareholders.

Independent members of the board are less apt to be 'yes men'. Directors with ties to management may be less willing or able to effectively evaluate and scrutinize company strategy and performance. Furthermore, boards without adequate independence from management may have other inherent conflicts of interest.

Also, there needs to be a balance between board refreshment, board stability, and the importance of some long-tenured directors to a company's success. Governance is only one part of a director's role and concern about extended board tenures and a preference for board refreshment can do more harm than good (see note below). Therefore, director tenure is an issue that is best left to boards to address individually.

*How to assess it?*

Look out for conflicts of interests between board members and the CEO found in the Related Party section of the proxy statement. Also ask the CEO how each of the directors came to the company. The latter should be accompanied by checking up the board members that have come to the business during the CEO´s tenure.

Typically, the CEO plays an important role in bringing board members in. If all of the directors were brought to the company by the CEO, it's fair to ask the CEO how confident an investor should be of the board's capacity to monitor their performance independently (one of the principal roles of all boards).

For Redeye to determine whether an appointed director is independent under our standards, the following minimum criteria for the director are required:

1) No fees received from the company (committee, consulting or board) are more than 20% in relation to their annual income;

2) No previous employment at the company;

3) No family relationships with the company's executives or directors;

4) No transactions between the director, the director's employer or the director's immediate family member's current employer and the company in the last fiscal year.

If more than 50% of the board members are considered independent, the stock is scored one point.

NOTE: Typically, listing standards state that for a director to be independent no or only a minor share of ownership is allowed, nor should the director have any relationship to a significant shareholder. Warren Buffett mentioned that Jesus understood this calibration of independence far more than most institutions. Matthew 6:21 observes: "For where your treasure is, there will your heart be also." We stick to Buffett's biblical standard when it comes to independence and ownership. We believe that a meaningful level of share ownership is a good sign, but not necessary for independence.

Similarly, the least independent directors tend to be those who receive an important fraction of their annual income from fees they receive for board service (and who also hope as well to be recommended for election to other boards and thereby to boost their income further). Yet these are the very board members most often classed as 'independent'. While pay should be sufficient to attract high-calibre individuals, directors with disproportionately high fees are deemed not independent by our standards.

Another issue with listing standards is long-tenured directors. When a company limits a competent director's term, it limits his or her opportunity to learn and acquire relevant expertise to contribute to more than just governing. Directors need to provide long-term strategic guidance to management, by coaching and nurturing talent. The prospect of investing a huge amount of time to learn the business and win management's trust and respect is daunting. For most directors this is a long journey, and it would be unwise to kick them out after they've served for several years. After all, companies don't fire high-performance employees on their tenth anniversary.

Moreover, if the board is composed of members with prestige, political figures, close friends, consultants, or lawyers, this may indicate that the CEO is bringing in people loyal to him or her and is not running the business with shareholders' interests in mind. However, there may be good reasons behind such choices, so be sure to do further investigation to find out. For example, a challenging regulatory climate might be a good reason to have a lawyer at the table.

## 2. Does the board hold regular meetings without the CEO to review his or her performance?

*Why does it matter?*

All CEOs should be measured according to a set of performance standards. Yet the CEO's performance is harder to measure than that of most workers. A terrible manager is a lot easier to confront or remove than a mediocre manager.

A key problem in all governance structures is that evaluation of CEOs is never conducted in regular meetings in the absence of that chief executive. Holding regular meetings without the CEO to review his or her performance can produce marked improvements in corporate governance. If there are concerns, the board should try to help develop the CEO unless it becomes objectively clear that he or she cannot do the job and must be replaced.

*How to assess it?*

Contact the chairman of the board or the remuneration committee and ask if they hold regular annual meetings without the CEO (and directors who are members of management) to review his or her performance. Try to verify this by checking up meeting attendance at the remuneration committee in the annual report.

Ask the CEO how confident an investor should be that the board is suitably independent to monitor his or her performance and what performance standards he or she is being measured on. The latter should be set by the board's outside directors and tailored to the particular business and corporate culture, but stress fundamental baselines such as returns on shareholder capital and steady progress in market value per share.

Likewise, ask if the board also has a contingency plan that is updated regularly and is ready to be put into action at short notice. This typically includes meetings without the CEO to discuss who would be called on to serve as acting CEO in the event of the current CEO becoming unable to function for any reason.

If the board holds regular meetings without the CEO to review his or her performance, the stock is scored one point.

### 3. Is the size of the board reasonable?

*Why does it matter?*

Board size is an important factor in board performance because the effectiveness of each director is strongly influenced by the number of other directors with whom each director must interact. Boards must be small enough to promote timely discussion and efficient decision-making, but also large enough to gain sufficient input and encourage debate. A board that is too small or too large tends to be easy for management to control.

A director on a board with too many members will find it very difficult to participate in the full board's leadership process and outcomes, which includes intense listening, thought-provoking questioning, and insightful comments and perspectives. Also, larger boards typically lead to less candid discussion of managerial performance and to greater control by the CEO.

A director on a board with too few members will experience isolation, limited input, interaction with a narrow field of vision, and pressure to reduce his or her independence. Moreover, the board may be too tightly knit to have diverse perspectives. And if the board is composed of an even number of directors, it will have more trouble reaching consensus.

*How to assess it?*

At least five directors are needed to effectively staff the standing committees required in regulated markets: the audit, compensation and nominating/governance committees. But more than nine directors would be too many.

If the board has five to nine members (excluding members of executive management), the stock is scored one point.

## 4. Do most board directors appear business-savvy and shareholder-oriented?

*Why does it matter?*

Many investors view the board of directors' calibre as a proxy for the company's quality. The validation that comes with respected board members means other investors are far more likely to consider investing in the business, but great directors are rare.

Directors need to be big-picture strategic thinkers, with thought and principles guiding their actions – not rules. They typically exhibit strong business acumen and are most likely professional high-performers themselves.

Business-savvy directors often improve company performance by acting as respected mentors for the management team. They help where they can and when they can't they make introductions to the right resources.

Another important aspect of a board is shareholder-orientation. Directors will be most inclined to look out for shareholders' interests when they are shareholders themselves – the higher the stake, the more passionate the stewardship. Such directors are committed to creating long-term value.

Conversely, a lack of business-savvy and shareholder-orientated directors can result in terribly over-priced acquisitions, strategy blunders and hiring mistakes.

*How to assess it?*

Look for directors who are business-savvy and shareholder-oriented and arrive with a strong specific interest in the company. Warren Buffett has often noted the advantage that companies gain from this kind of director. To determine whether each board member is a good fit according to these standards, you should review all directors' professional background and speak with them in person if possible.

Whether a board director is considered *business-savvy* or not depends on whether they have a very successful capital allocation and/or operational track record. The former includes deep experience of the capital markets and fund raising, but primarily involves a great track record of long-term investing. The latter means that they have helped (as a director, manager or major shareholder) build or maintain a successful business over an extended period while providing superior returns to owners. The key here is that the director understands what constitutes a high-quality business – this is an absolute necessity.

Not only must board members be business savvy, but they must also be *shareholder-oriented*. It is desirable that they hold sizeable personal stakes in companies they serve, above and beyond board compensation, so that they truly walk in the owners' shoes. These holdings should not be acquired via options or grants. After all, a good reason why someone should consider joining a company's board is to invest a significant portion of their net worth and be able to watch it closely.

Lastly, a willingness to make a significant equity investment in the company should be considered confirmation of a strong interest in the company. This typically means that directors are willing to commit their time and work hard. They take board meetings very seriously. Check board attendance as it indicates whether they are fulfilling their obligation to represent shareholders and provide management with oversight and direction. Attendance of less than 80% of all board and committee meetings over the last couple of years would suggest further investigation is needed.

If more than 50% of the board members are considered business savvy and shareholder-oriented, the stock is scored one point.

NOTE: Ideally a director has professional experience directly related to the company's business, either as an entrepreneur or as an executive or director in a high-performing company. At the same time, however, it is important to recognise that some of the best ideas, insights and contributions can come from directors whose professional experiences are not directly related to the company's business.

**5. Is the company free of abuses of power for personal gain?**

*Why does it matter?*

If the board members or senior executives are using their positions to enrich themselves, friends or relatives, it can bring their integrity into question. For example, if any supplier is related to the board of directors or management it is possible that they might not be receiving the best price for the goods or services. This conflict of interest could be hurting the bottom line.

Some related-party transactions can actually be good for business. That is not to say we should ignore this, but rather recognise the need for careful assessment of the people you entrust with your money. But beware situations that could lead to conflicts of interest. It could be any board or management team member that previously has done something self-serving that appears dumb.

*How to assess it?*

Do a search for the term 'related party' in the annual report and read the paragraphs. The key here is to make sure that the company isn't sending a significant amount of business to related parties. Also watch out for any flagrant pattern of abuse of power where insiders treat the company as their piggy bank. A warning sign should also be assigned if the company doesn't disclose information on related party transactions, or if it faces legal challenges.

One of the worst kinds of related-party transactions is money lent to insiders to purchase company stock. Another bad one is when the CEO owns the building and leases it back to the company.

If the company is devoid of any abuse of power for personal gain, the stock is scored one point.

## 6. Does the chairman serve on an excessive number of outside boards?

*Why does it matter?*

As for other non-executives, but even more so for the chairman of the board, holding multiple outside board positions and other commitments may represent an impediment to the director's ability to devote sufficient time to the needs of each company.

*How to assess it?*

In this check we consider over-boarding. We look at the total number of board seats (including the company) held by the chairman to determine if it's excessive, defined as more than four public company board seats and a maximum of two chairman positions. Moreover, as a chairman they should not hold an executive position in order to maintain appropriate focus and not be distracted by competing responsibilities.

If the chairman serves on more than four public company board seats (including the company) and holds more than two chairman positions, this check is flagged:

This factor has a zero-weight impact on the scoring model for People and is included as additional information to assist with investment decision-making.

# BUSINESS TENETS

## DOES THE BUSINESS HAVE FAVOURABLE LONG-TERM PROSPECTS?

# BACKGROUND

If you don't understand the competitive environment and don't have a clear sense of how the business will engage customers, create value and consistently deliver that value at a profit, you won't succeed as an investor. The key is to identify the factors that will produce future earnings and be able to make a reliable forecast of them. Considering these factors in depth is much more valuable than reading the most recent quarterly report.

The most common source for uncovering potential growth drivers is the annual report. Through it you can gain an overview of the company's core business, understand how it makes money and assess which drivers kept the business growing over the past few years. It also reveals future expansion plans. It is also wise to read competitors' annual reports to gain a more nuanced view of the market.

## THE FRAMEWORK

The Business rating is based on quantitative scores grouped into six sub-categories: Business Scalability, Market Structure,

Value Proposition, Competitive Moat, Operational Risks, and Social Responsibility.

All of these sub-categories are assessed on five checks of quantitative and qualitative questions. Each check is allocated one point if the question can be answered with a 'Yes'; the total number of these points makes up each sub-category's score on a scale that ranges from 0 to 5 rounded to the nearest whole number. If unsure about a question or disclosure is inadequate, the check fails by default. This is consistent with the best ideas often being the simplest.

Each sub-category also includes a sixth complementary check. These negative questions provide additional information to assist with investment decision-making, but have no impact on the scoring model.

# BUSINESS SCALABILITY ANALYSIS

IS THE BUSINESS MODEL REPEATABLE AND SCALABLE?

When businesses are highly successful, one of the common key ingredients is scalability. A scalable business model is the most important way in which rapid and sustained growth can take place. Businesses with high scalability grow with lower capital requirements, making them more efficient and more attractive to investors. Scaling simply means that the business has the potential to multiply revenue with minimal incremental cost.

Look for a business model that shows the path to growth and profits very clearly. Be sure to understand what they do and how they plan to succeed. The more certain you can be of future cash flows, the higher premium you will put on a business, and as a result, you will see a higher valuation.

A high margin, recurring revenues and low capital requirements lead to stable and predictable free cash flows. Moreover, subscriptions are generally more predictable and reliable and as a result create more investor confidence leading to higher multiples and more valuable businesses.

Avoid business models that are difficult to decode. Be wary of management teams that imply that their superior intelligence overcompensates for the complexity of their business models. Opaque business models are often an invitation to a scandal or shareholder lawsuit.

If you can't understand how a business makes money, then you should stay away. It's really important to focus on 'easy to scale' because that enables 'fast to scale'.

## BUSINESS SCALABILITY CHECKLIST

1. Are a major portion of existing or potential revenues recurring?
2. Does the company have strategic alliances that can help drive its total sales?
3. Is the business asset-light and able to scale up without expensive reinvestment?
4. Is strategy focused on organic growth?
5. Does the company have a history of successful expansion into new markets or locations?
6. *Is this a pre-revenue company which hasn't yet proven its business model?*

∼

**1. Are a major portion of existing or potential revenues recurring?**

*Why does it matter?*

A high degree of recurring revenues increases the stability of a business and the predictability of its cash flows. Businesses with multiple sources of recurring revenue almost always have big premiums to their valuation multiples because of their predictability.

*How to assess it?*

Find out if the majority of the company's existing or potential revenues are predictable and recurring. Look for business models that support long-term, annuity-like, revenue streams with the following characteristics:

1. repeatable offering based on long-term contracted revenues like subscription, training, maintenance, leasing, or license fees;

2. repeat use of the product based on short repurchase cycles like aftermarket sales (disposables, for example) or products bought out of habit.

The first characteristic means the customer is renting the product, not owning it. The second means that the product is consumed daily or weekly by customers and will need to be purchased again quickly, no matter how the economy is doing.

Nonetheless, not all recurring revenues are equal. The biggest potential issue is if the customer is being charged based on usage or transactions, which could deviate significantly. It's very important to understand the quality and volatility of the 'recurring' revenue and the difference between annuity income streams and lumpy revenues.

For example, software companies can sell a one-time license that includes the first year of support. After that, the customer often pays about 20% of the license as part of a recurring maintenance revenue.

But software can also be sold as a subscription in which both the license and maintenance fees are embedded into the subscription fee. Such subscription businesses take longer to grow than traditional software businesses, but once they reach scale investors put premium multiples on their more predictable future revenue streams.

This is particularly true for automatic renewals of 'evergreen' subscriptions like software maintenance or phone service, as these often continue through inertia rather than by contract.

If more than 50% of the company's existing or potential revenues appear to be recurring, the stock is scored one point.

## 2. Does the company have strategic alliances that can help drive its total sales?

*Why does it matter?*

This check evaluates whether the company has a strategic partner that adds real value to its product offering. The main objective of strategic alliances is to sharpen competitive edge in relation to other companies, and as such they can add value to the customer relationship that increase the stickiness of those relationships.

Teaming up with others adds complementary resources and capabilities, enabling participants to grow and expand more quickly and efficiently. Especially fast-growing companies rely heavily on alliances to extend their technical and operational resources. In the process, they save time and boost productivity by not having to develop their own, from scratch. They are thus freed to concentrate on innovation and their core business.

*How to assess it?*

Evaluate if the company has a strategic alliance (partnership, technology licensing agreement or joint venture) that strengthens the offering by adding value recognizable to its customers. Hence it must strengthen the offering's value proposition to customers.

If the company has a strategic partner that adds real value to its offering, the stock is scored one point.

### 3. Is the business asset-light and able to scale up without expensive reinvestment?

*Why does it matter?*

This check evaluates if the company is able to finance its growth itself. More precisely, it examines whether it is asset-light as this enables it to expand faster, more easily and on a larger scale. Such companies can generate more cash while growing, and due to low capital investment, there is no need for borrowing, and the overall business risk is much lower. Moreover, a low asset base leads to lower volatility in earnings and is simpler to value, so is generally valued more highly than an asset-heavy business.

Ideally a company doesn't own much of the physical assets. Instead it makes use of other companies' investments for its own benefit. It may outsource some of the production and/or services, license in and out through strategic alliances, and asset-share. Usually it has developed a single product that it can sell to a lot of customers with few incremental costs.

The very best businesses often find a way to leverage someone else's capital expenditures for free (the upfront cost of connecting people to the web, for example). Typically, such companies leverage technology substantially to provide their business with rapid scalability, significant efficiencies, and great profitability.

If large capital investments are required to manufacture products or to provide services, the business is capital-intensive. It requires constant funding, and a lot more to grow, which will either dilute shareholders (through additional equity raises) or use up earned cash. Examples of capital-intensive industries are automobile manufacturing, airlines, steel production, oil production and refining, and chemicals production.

*How to assess it?*

An asset-light business model is one that requires little capital for operations and expansion. Two common turnover ratios to use in your assessment of whether a business is asset-light are sales to working capital and sales to fixed assets.

Working capital turnover serves as a good measure of operating efficiency. The higher the working capital turnover, the less money a company has tied up to achieve its sales. Working capital is simply the money needed to keep 'oiling the wheels' of the business. If the working capital turnover ratio is 5 or higher it is considered asset-light, but the best companies actually have negative working capital. It is common to see negative working capital in subscription-based business models where customers pay up for recurring service or access. Because revenue is recognized when the service is performed, which is after the cash comes in, these businesses typically have operating cash flow that exceeds net profit.

Likewise, turnover of fixed assets (property, plant, and equipment, or PPE) is a good proxy for a company's capital intensity. Companies with low capital intensity typically have small fixed asset bases resulting in a high turnover ratio above 5, as it implies a relatively modest physical asset base.

For example, if a typical manufacturing business wants to grow it will require significant capital investments in new factories, machinery, and trucks. However, what you should be looking for is a scalable business that makes money based on intangible assets such as brand name, intellectual property, or developed technology.

As turnover ratios typically fluctuate from year to year, look at the average over five years to get an accurate picture.

If the business appears asset-light and able to scale up without expensive reinvestment, the stock is scored one point.

## 4. Is strategy focused on organic growth?

*Why does it matter?*

Ideally, you want a growth strategy that is more dependent on organic margin improvement initiatives than market share gains by frenetic acquisition activity, as a growth-by-acquisition strategy makes the company more difficult to understand.

Typically, organic growth (or same-store growth) is long-term in nature whereas growth by acquisitions gives companies incremental gains in the shorter term. The advantage of the organic route of growth is a consistency in the growth path, a lack of turbulence and the ability to chart and structure the company's future activities.

A growth-by-acquisition strategy involves more complex accounting that can more easily conceal problems. In addition, each acquisition typically ends up being bigger than the last, increasing the price and therefore the level of risk.

Another issue with acquisitions is that integrating excessive purchases can be distracting for management and disruptive to the acquirer's core business as it often tends to dilute the culture. The classic example of this pitfall is Coca-Cola in the 1980s, which allocated proceeds from the core business into acquiring Columbia Studios before refocusing a few years later. However, serial acquirers are a different breed of companies than companies that make large 'transformative' deals. For more, please see check #4 in the Capital Allocation checklist on page 79.

Although acquisitions can be entirely reasonable, the experience of most companies across the world shows that organic growth is generally the wiser choice when it comes to building up a business. But once critical mass is achieved, a successful acquisition can help that company grow further and increase the core business's competitive advantage.

*How to assess it?*

Managers should always describe the strategy that will shape the company's future, it should be easy to find along with its key assumptions on its homepage and annual reports. Keep in mind, that high levels of capital spending and rapid increases in market share are often tell-tale signs of a deal mania and a management racing out of control.

If there is a strategy to mainly grow the business under its own power, the stock is scored one point.

## 5. Does the company have a history of successful expansion into new markets or locations?

*Why does it matter?*

Expansion stories are great. They show that the company has a business model that works and can be adapted to different geographies or locations. Past success with geographic expansion can be a good indicator of future success.

Geographic expansion is one of the most challenging strategies for any businesses to implement, where failed attempts are legion and can prove damaging to the original franchise. Products that work well in the home market do not necessarily translate to success in a new market but have to be reformulated to appeal to this market.

*How to assess it?*

Look for companies that have proven that they are capable of successfully replicating their success by exporting their competitive advantages into new geographical areas or multiple locations. Such companies have typically proved that they have reliable infrastructure in place to scale and match the rate of growth in demand.

Advantages that derive from a unique distribution system, localised scale advantages, or favourable regulatory treatment may not be replicated abroad.

Adaptability is often the result of considerable trial and error and takes time. Indeed, companies that rely on unique business structures for competitive advantage at home will face the greatest difficulty expanding geographically.

If the company has a history of successful expansion into new markets, the stock is scored one point.

## 6. Is this a pre-revenue company which hasn't yet proven its business model?

*Why does it matter?*

There is a major difference between a pre- and post-revenue company, and this huge leap is often not fully captured in the increase in valuation from the former to the latter stage. Getting a customer to actually pay for something is a major milestone, an indication that the company is building a product that a customer in its target market finds valuable. Before that first sale is made, it's all just speculation.

*How to assess it?*

Look at the income statement to determine whether the company has product sales, i.e. a proven product or established market fit. Beware any one-time payments related to licensing etc. as they are not product sales.

If this company hasn't yet proven its business model, this check is flagged:

This factor has a zero-weight impact on the scoring model for Business and is included as additional information to assist with investment decision-making.

# MARKET STRUCTURE ANALYSIS

DOES THE BUSINESS OPERATE IN A FAVOURABLE MARKET STRUCTURE?

Assessing a company's market structure is essential as it is a major factor that affects its future profitability. Markets where industry dynamics have been substantially unchanged and competition relatively rational over many years are more likely to remain that way. The greater the number of rivals, the easier it is for new competitors to enter the market and the more rapidly technology changes, the more difficult it is to sustain success.

Similarly, slow-growing markets are generally preferable as they don't attract competitors. History support this as many of the best-performing investments are found in shrinking and slower growing industries, but only if the business has lots of room for expansion with a differentiated (and often disruptive) product. All the same, it's challenging to achieve predictable growth when the pie is shrinking – even if the company is the leader and taking market share.

In terms of industry structure an oligopoly is preferred to a fragmented competitive landscape. That means market conditions with just a few competitors where all are highly profitable and protected by strong barriers to entry and scaling. This translates into a stable market with few new players.

Nothing lasts forever and change is the only thing you can count on. Yet many investors fail to think carefully enough about competition and obsolescence as they typically confuse novelty with disruptive innovation. But where there is disruption there's also opportunity. Therefore it's critical to keep an eye on the major innovation trends of the future.

## MARKET STRUCTURE CHECKLIST

1. Does the business have a long runway for growth?
2. Does the business operate in a highly profitable industry?
3. Does the business operate in a slow-changing market with long product cycles?
4. Does the business have limited competition?
5. Is the business resilient in the face of new innovations?
6. *Does the company make an exciting product or operate in a sexy industry?*

∼

**1. Does the business have a long runway for growth?**

*Why does it matter?*

This check assesses whether the company has products with sufficient market potential to enable substantial increases in sales over a decade at least. A company seeking a sustained period of growth needs to have plenty of room to continue reinvesting capital both organically and through acquisitions for years into the future. Developing insights about a company's growth potential is clearly critical for predictability.

*How to assess it?*

Look for an end-market that is primed for an indefinite period of growth ahead. Instead of focusing on next quarter or next year, the key is to step back and envision how big this company can be in a decade or two. What you are looking for is the certainty that the company has the ability to grow consistently for many years to come, preferably decades. Often this means that the company has products that address large and growing markets, rather than shrinking ones with substantial over-capacity.

Think about the runway left and total addressable market (often referred to as TAM) for a company. The lower the degree of market penetration, the greater the remaining growth potential for a company. Don't just project growth rates from the past into the future as very few companies can keep growing for decades. That's why you should try to assess if the company's product pipeline has good sales potential compared to existing products to extend growth after its current products have matured.

What is often missed is positive optionality. You should always be thinking about the company's current products' optionality for other markets – revenue streams that are yet to be tapped. Think of how Amazon has transformed from a bookseller to the all-encompassing retailer that it is today, as well as a leading cloud services company. To find out if the company benefits from positive optionality you should ask yourself two questions: what can the company become? And what does its current business make possible? It could be substantial scope of geographic expansion, extensions in terms of product range, potential to increase penetration of its product, potential to gain market share, opportunity to consolidate an industry through acquisitions etc.

If the company is competing in a completely new market, try to estimate market size and adoption rates for this new market. Also try to understand the impact from current mega-trends (profound changes in economic conditions that occur over the long term) as these play a critical role in how large a market can become and how quickly.

However, always be cautious if management's definition of TAM is overly broad, as they may be trying to mislead investors. Similarly, you should be wary if a company that claims to have a long runway begins shifting into new or different markets. The company should primarily be selling more of the same product while producing consistent unit economics. Yet, many businesses start with a bang but are in a market that lacks a big runway.

If it's possible to imagine the company at five times the scale it currently operates at in a decade from now, the stock is scored one point. Of course, this level of conviction is very rare, but it is an essential ingredient for compounders.

## 2. Does the business operate in a highly profitable industry?

*Why does it matter?*

This check measures the attractiveness of the industry in which a company operates. A large part of your potential rate of return over the long-term is attributable to the industry you are invested in, as opposed to a specific company you are invested in. This criterion helps you to determine which companies are in the most promising industries for you as an investor.

The profitability of a business typically trends toward the mean of the industry, as it is difficult for any business to outperform the industry for a long period of time. Any business can earn above-average return for a while, but competition eventually compels most businesses to pass the savings along to consumers. Likewise, it takes a truly exceptional business to buck a trend of challenging conditions.

*How to assess it?*

In order to assess whether the business operates in a highly profitable industry, check whether the industry's 10-year median ROIC is greater than 15%. To refine expectations, you could dig down to more refined sub-industry groupings.

If it's easy to make money in an industry, you will find that most companies are doing well, and the best businesses are not far from the worst in terms of return on invested capital (ROIC). Indirectly a high ROIC for the relevant industry will also answer if the company's strategy and those of its rivals are more focused on profitability than market share.

However, be careful when buying into an industry with excess capacity since overcapacity is normally equated with negative or below average ROIC. Similarly, you should be cautious if the management tend to talk about their peers in disrespectful terms. If the language used is dismissive or aggressive, the risk of mutually destructive behaviour increases.

If the 10-year median ROIC for the relevant industry is greater than 15%, the stock is scored one point.

## 3. Does the business operate in a slow-changing market with long product cycles?

*Why does it matter?*

This check indicates whether the company operates in a slow changing market, as consistent products equate to consistent profits. Some businesses have significantly longer life spans than others due to the nature of their products. Companies whose products have long product cycles, that last for more than a decade, don't have to continually invent new technologies and keep competing with new generations of products. Or more precisely, they are more adaptable because they have more time to see and react to change.

Many investing mistakes arise from illusions of predictability, which are especially acute in a rapidly changing industry. A short product cycle means that it is much easier for a new player to come in and do better. So, sustaining market leadership in industries marked by fast-paced innovation is extremely challenging.

Companies that are resilient to technological innovation are becoming increasingly harder to find as technology impacts more and more industries. In fast-changing markets companies must stay flexible and keep an eye on the needs of the constantly evolving markets they operate in. Any competitive advantage has to come from a corporate culture, the ability to constantly come up with new or improved products, rather than the products themselves. Nonetheless, at some point companies that must change constantly are destined to make wrong decisions and succumb.

*How to assess it?*

It is consistency in the product that creates consistency in the company profits. Look for opportunities where time is an ally, not an enemy. If you think that the company will continue to sell the same or similar products for the next 10 years, then the business is considered as operating in a slow-changing market with long product cycles. Typically, you will see a gradual product improvement over time that discourage competitors from entering.

A good complementary sign is if the industry market shares have remained stable with few new players in the last five years, as market share volatility is a sign of weak entry and/or scaling barriers.

Think of the smartphone market. Apple never produced phones when BlackBerry was the king of the smartphone market. In 2009 Blackberry was producing incredibly high returns on invested capital of around 40%. But just five years later Blackberry was a completely different business with different products than it was in 2009. The bottom line is that you should avoid companies that are dependent on evolving technology adoption along with a hypercompetitive marketplace as obsolescence risk is high.

If you judge that the company will continue to sell the same or similar products for the next 10 years, the stock is scored one point.

## 4. Does the business have limited competition?

*Why does it matter?*

Competition always exists but does not increase the value of a business. Generally, more competition means more customer choice and less profitability. In addition, a business with limited competition is more predictable than one that has lots of competitors.

Everyone has competition, even those companies that are disrupting a market. Even so, some competition is acceptable because competitors help educate the market. Competitors' presence can also legitimise and reduce the perceived risk of a new product category and attract enabling services and technologies.

*How to assess it?*

To understand the nature of the competitive landscape, check whether companies have a history of co-existing peacefully with each other, making the industry highly profitable overall as a result. This is most likely to exist if there are only a few companies that talk about each other in respectful terms.

A great sign is if the industry is consolidated to just a handful of players of various sizes with entirely different value propositions for customers. As a result, all diverge away from competing on common ground. Likewise, any sign of capacity leaving the industry is likely to be highly positive for future returns.

If you can list the company's competitors by name, it is considered to have limited competition, and the stock is scored one point.

## 5. Is the business resilient in the face of new innovations?

*Why does it matter?*

Beware companies operating in areas at the leading edge of technology. When it comes to competition it is key to think not about where the company is competing, but where it is going to be competing. This is particularly important in industries where the pace of technological change is very fast, like healthcare and technology.

A change in market or industry structure is a major opportunity for innovation. Technological changes driving market alterations are often more serious than they initially seem. Large, dominant producers and suppliers, having been successful and unchallenged for many years, tend to be arrogant and slow to respond.

At first, they dismiss the newcomer as insignificant and, indeed, amateurish. But even when the newcomer takes a larger and larger share of their business, they typically find it hard to mobilize themselves for counteraction. The bottom line is that companies in industries that have changed rapidly survive only if they keep renewing themselves at a fast pace. They either get research priorities right or competition leaves them in the dust. Think Nokia versus Apple.

*How to assess it?*

All listed companies around the world must provide commentary about their performance and outlook on a regular basis. There you'll find clues about where they see threats coming from. From there you can dig further to discover the emerging players in their market and how they get a piece of the action in order to understand the threat from new innovations.

It's important to understand that very meaningful competition can come not only from similar products but also doing it an entirely different way, or even not doing it at all. Try to escape the present and project some of the more obvious new behaviours and technologies farther out into the future. New enabling technologies are often leading indicators of where the next great wave of innovation can be created, as most technological advances are widely applicable to many problems and markets. Moreover, the biggest opportunity for disruption typically is in markets where you see a lot of advertising, as it signals that existing players can't rely on product differentiation. In general, the industries that have proven the most vulnerable to disruption have been those with:

- One or a few major players
- Relatively outdated business practices
- Slow technology adoption

Always ask yourself if a bigger company (Apple or Amazon, for example) can easily harness this opportunity and steal market share away (often by offering free products)? For example, dozens of businesses were eaten by the smartphone with its sensors, always-on connectivity and powerfully flexible user interfaces. Never forget that the value proposition for any technology is to do more with less.

In business, being superb and easy to use matters more than being first. Technology almost always moves quickly, but changes in customer behaviour almost never do until they reach a critical tipping point. Look for signs of new technologies that foster product improvements and whether there has been a shift to horizontal markets from an industry organized vertically.

Don't confuse novelty with disruptive innovation. The former is more a question of great features added in an attempt to differentiate, whereas real innovation redefines the market as it changes the way the world works. Typically, it transforms complex and expensive products by deploying new technology or business model to make them easier, cheaper or more convenient. This happens in part because the disruptor accepts lower margins and pursues a specific piece of the value chain that incumbents neglected. And in part because the innovation does not fit into the incumbents' established way of making money, preventing them from commercialising it. Disruptive innovation simply is reinvention that is industry-altering.

Services are generally less prone to disruption through obsolescence as they are typically competing on a local geographical scale, while products tend to compete on a global basis. Similarly, companies with sophisticated, or complex, products are more likely to fend off competition for a longer time, as the technical challenge of replicating products creates high barriers to entry. Moreover, such companies probably possess technological expertise that can be applied to next-generation products. Protection from competition is particularly strong with companies that require both hard engineering and operational knowledge to scale.

If the market is safe from new, competing technology or innovations that threaten the business, the stock is scored one point.

NOTE: Keep in mind that great innovations tend to follow patterns, face similar growth rates, obstacles to growth, and so on. Cars at first had no highways and gas stations, telegraphs had no poles and wires, the internet had no broadband. Try to learn by studying how the great entrepreneurs dealt with such challenges, how technology evolved, and how they got disrupted in turn by newer ideas.

### 6. Does the company make an exciting product or operate in a sexy industry?

*Why does it matter?*

The market typically pays an entertainment tax or a premium for stocks with an exciting story. It's easy to invest in dreams. People often look for excitement when investing in the stock market, but that's not where the money typically is. This may seem counter-intuitive, but a boring industry is good. It doesn't attract attention and this ability to keep out of sight of potential competitors is an advantage, a sort of 'security by obscurity'.

This relative obscurity can offer a layer of protection from competitive disruption, as it generally won't be a hotly-contested market environment. Likewise, such companies typically receive a lot less scrutiny from investors. This makes fertile grounds for you to find unanticipated growth. At the end of the day, you want a company that makes money more than one in a sexy industry.

On the other hand, people may buy the stock because they believe its price can become detached from the fundamentals or economics of the business. In these situations, incremental earnings may be worth many times more for sexy products than if the company made some mundane product. Such 'story' stocks typically carry a lot of volatility, something that gives the opportunity to buy at low prices and sell at high prices. The key to successful investing in story stocks is to discover them before the crowd does and they go viral, attracting the momentum trading community.

*How to assess it?*

A boring product is typically the same as a 'simple-to-understand' product. The same goes for companies that operate in a boring-sounding industry. Such companies rarely make the business headlines and are likely to have lower price volatility. Also, boring companies are often suppliers for others or sell everyday products that people continue to buy regardless of how the economy is doing.

If the company either makes an exciting product or operates in a sexy industry, this check is flagged.

This factor has a zero-weight impact on the scoring model for Business and is included as additional information to assist with investment decision-making.

# VALUE PROPOSITION ANALYSIS

DO THE PRODUCTS PROVIDE
UNIQUE AND DESIRED BENEFITS
TO CUSTOMERS?

How badly customers want their product is a key driver of how profitable a company is. As long as a company is valued by its customers, its value will be retained. Providing a stand-out product is the key to success, which is the same as delivering a great customer value proposition.

The value proposition helps the company to differentiate itself from competitors and to focus on providing core value for customers. For any company to succeed it has to be designed from the outside in, based on what the customers really want and need, rather than inside out, based on strategic objectives and financial goals.

One of the main pitfalls in researching a business lies in viewing the business from your own perspective, instead of viewing the business from the customer perspective. Your personal preferences are irrelevant to investing. In the end, from a shareholder perspective, value is what the customers pay for.

A company that lack a value proposition is just a commoditised business and will have to compete on price and price alone. Yet, in many industries, differentiation simply can't be made meaningful. In such industries a company needs to race for cost leadership as commodity products tend to get priced by the marginal producer's cost of production.

## VALUE PROPOSITION CHECKLIST

1. Does the company have a focused core group of customers?
2. Do the products solve a genuine customer need, rather than create desire?
3. Are the products only modestly vulnerable to substitutes?
4. Does the company offer good value to its customers?
5. Does the development process take place in close co-operation with paying customers?
6. *Is constant heavy spending on marketing required for growth?*

∾

### 1. Does the company have a focused core group of customers?

*Why does it matter?*

Different customers typically have widely varying needs. Knowing who the core or target customers of the business are is key to gaining in-depth understanding of a business, their position and to monitor customer trends and how the business caters to them. The more focused a customer group a company has, the better it is able to appeal to those customers and manage for their loyalty.

Many times, it's just a small percentage of customers that represent a large percentage of the revenues for a business. As a result, a company's true market is typically limited to those customers for whom that purchase is a top buying priority (the ideal customer). As you go up in customer buying priorities, you generally go down in market size, since more people feel a problem generally than acutely.

Focus taken to the extreme, can easily put a company in a situation where it's building a product for a single unique customer. In other words, the probability of failure goes up exponentially as the number of product features increase.

*How to assess it?*

Beware those businesses that attempt to cater to too many types of customers with the exact same product, as there are no 'average' customers. Instead, make sure that the company has a clearly defined core (target) customer segment. To identify the core customer, ask management questions like: If you could allocate more resources to one specific group who would it be? Which customers are the most loyal? Among which customers is the brand's recognition most widespread?

If core customers generate at least two thirds of a company's revenues, which is twice as much as the rest of the company's operations combined, the stock is scored one point.

NOTE: Keep in mind that customer need is a continuum, and that the real difference between the need-to-have and nice-to-have customers is just a market size question and a question about buying priorities. There are always more mainstream customers who will buy but view the product as nice-to-have rather than need-to-have.

As the company moves beyond early adopters into mainstream markets, the company must adjust and reposition its product offering again and again to meet the needs of an expanded market. Typically, early adopters buy the core product, but the mainstream is interested in offerings that meet a broader set of requirements that often demand complementary products. The latter comes at the risk of losing focus, as the company expands its product lines.

## 2. Do the products solve a genuine customer need, rather than create desire?

*Why does it matter?*

The best businesses are so good at solving problems for their customers that they become indispensable. Many new products serve a useful purpose, but they don't change our lives or our productivity in a meaningful way. There's simply no point in making a product that brings no real substantial value to customers.

Consider the common everyday fidget spinner – the low-friction plastic toy that seemingly defies Newton's laws. They were wanted badly by many, yet weren't great investments for their manufacturers in the long run. The distinction is that a valuable company provides a product that is useful and will remain valued by its customers.

*How to assess it?*

You have to get into the mindset of a future buyer to understand how useful this new product will be or how well the product is plugged into the customer's value chain. The key is to assess whether or not there is long-term demand for the company's product. Products hold their primacy just so long as their quality remains high.

Look for products that improve health, enrich emotional life, fulfill basic needs or is perceived as necessary, but where customers can't or won't switch. If the product is a default choice for most customers, it's probably a need-to-have item. The holy grail is a product that is lifestyle-changing as it can achieve 'hockey-stick' earnings trajectory for at least a few years. Also, when a product gives the consumer a competitive advantage, it will usually see very rapid uptake as it becomes established as a new industry standard.

A great product/market fit strongly tends to generate strong word of mouth. If you are solving a real need in someone's life, it's only natural that they will talk to other people about it. However, be cautious if the company's products are trend-sensitive or taste-dependent (fashion, flavours and fragrances, for example) as these are susceptible to shifting consumer preferences.

Customer loyalty is best understood by customer feedback, not by extrapolating past numbers. This makes it harder to estimate revenues using only historical numbers. Ask what customers would do without the company's products. If it was taken from them, would that be a problem? Would their life be worse?

Likewise, it is easy to be misled by good acquisition numbers when it comes to digital products. If the product has real value for customers, you should see good engagement numbers and even better retention metrics. Top-of-funnel growth means nothing if the users churn. Merely selling a product doesn't automatically translate into customer success – customer retention is a better indicator of future growth.

Provided there is a consistent flow of new customers at an acceptable acquisition cost, low churn will allow recurring revenues to grow – improving the growth rate and reducing the risk of value loss over the long term. A high churn rate has the opposite effects and can also signal to investors that the product does not meet the customer's needs adequately or sits in a market with limited demand or is competing with stronger products. This would imply that it requires further development at their expense. What churn rate is acceptable comes down in large part to which customer segment the business is targeting. As a rule of thumb, smaller customers tend to have higher churn rates.

Also, it's important to determine whether it's a technology which is not yet a product, or a product feature (or component supplier) which may never become more than an add-on for someone else's product, or if it's providing a complete solution or product concept that a substantial company can be built around.

If the company's product is likely to be in high demand far into the future, the stock is scored one point.

## 3. Are the products only modestly vulnerable to substitutes?

*Why does it matter?*

Customer perception is critical. With effective differentiation, a company minimizes the perception among consumers that its product has many close substitutes. Making products that offer proprietary content, have patented or unmatched features or acquiring and adding value to such products is a starting point for differentiation. In addition, a perceived lack of substitutes raises switching costs. That said, the most devastating substitutes cost less and have at least one feature that is superior.

*How to assess it?*

Try to assess whether the company's products are thought by its core customers to have no close substitutes. The key to answering this question is to understand why customers buy the company's product and why they might stop buying it or switch to a competitor's product.

A great way to learn interesting things about a company's product is to talk to the company's customers. Find out whether they are finding cheaper or simpler products that are 'good enough'? Can a customer perform similar functions with a different or more integrated product that appeals to potential customers who do not want multiple devices? Or would they have to own multiple devices or platforms to perform all of the necessary functions or have a similar experience?

A good complementary question is whether existing customers will stay even if a competitor lowers its price? Remember, the larger a corporate customer is, the more objective its purchasing decisions. Larger companies typically focus more on direct cost savings and are less willing to pay for intangible or convenience benefits. They typically use procurement departments that enhance rational behaviour in corporate buying.

If the company's products are thought by its customers to have no close substitute, the stock is scored one point.

## 4. Does the company offer good value to its customers?

*Why does it matter?*

Quality in a product is not what the supplier puts in - it's what the customer gets out and is willing to pay for. A business that wants to create value needs a unique and persuasive reason for its customers to buy. Often a marginal improvement on a marginal cost is not enough to drive buying behaviour in all but a tiny minority of power-users. Likewise, engineering doesn't always have the right answer because of the customer's subjective perception – especially for mission-critical products that are built on trust and reliability.

At the end of the day, customers are the stakeholders who determine the fate of a business. Sometimes they are unwilling to pay a premium price for a product, even if the less expensive alternative needs to be replaced or repaired frequently. Equally, if customers are not satisfied with a product they will eventually find alternatives, or another company will eventually create an alternative if one does not exist already.

*How to assess it?*

To convince customers to buy, new products usually need to be several orders of magnitude better than the current state of the art. There is a lot of inertia in the 'good enough' syndrome where people prefer the safe and familiar status quo. Moreover, the best product isn't always competitive on price as customers buy for other reasons as well, like cost and convenience or environmental concerns. Yet, it must be affordable for broad market adoption. That's why you should wait for a proof of customers' willingness to pay up for a product, which shows if it really offers them value. At earlier stages, accumulating a set of users who really loves it would be a great sign.

You should be highly concerned if a company seeks to extract as much value as possible from their customers in the attempt to maximize shareholder value. In these situations, customers will feel that they aren't getting good value. Sometimes they continue to pay because of limited competition, or the company having some form of competitive advantage. In that case the business is extracting value from, rather than adding value to, its customers. This parasitic relationship could lead to customers feeling exploited. If a competitor were to come up with a better alternative, they would probably jump ship.

Similarly, some companies create complexity for their customers because it makes things easier for themselves. Complexity comes in many forms: requiring customers to invest a lot of time learning how to use the product is one example. Other examples include requiring significant changes in their behaviour or, making it difficult for them to switch to another provider or, not being compatible with any products outside the selling company's own ecosystem. The last of these means the less optionality a business provides its customers, the less value the product will have for them. In all cases you should be very cautious if the company's product makes life harder for many customers, as creating a sales success is likely to be difficult.

Finally, beware your own blind spots when you don't match the user archetype that the company's product is built for. Since your personal preferences are irrelevant, always try talking to the company's customers to get a deep customer perspective.

If customers feel they get a good deal when they buy the company's products, the stock is scored one point.

## 5. Does the development process take place in close co-operation with paying customers?

*Why does it matter?*

You need to make sure there's a real demand for the company's products. When it comes to building products, success requires intense dedication to help client companies achieve their goals and solve their needs. An average company does not develop a deep enough understanding of customers' present and future needs and wants. Companies like this are at risk of being blindsided by shifting customer demands.

A business with a strong value proposition ultimately manages to ask its customers what they feel about the product, what they want to achieve and how they measure success and failure. Feelings and hidden motivations largely drive what we do, but they don't come with explanations attached. Still, most companies just ask customers what they want. The bottom line is that competitiveness is far more about doing what customers value than doing what the company thinks it's good at.

The best companies generally find ways to consistently engage the consumer and incorporate them into their innovation and planning initiatives – namely to spark ideas for improved or new products. Working closely with customers helps companies anticipate and meet or exceed their needs through data-driven foresight. Knowing exactly what customers and the customers' customer value enables a more effective development process, by minimising both product risk and time to market.

*How to assess it?*

Customer loyalty is best understood by customer feedback, not by extrapolating past numbers. Has the company shown a willingness to adapt to feedback quickly? Understanding the psychology of the customers requires a huge concentrated effort and investment.

Most companies have a 'financial fear factor' that keeps them from doing what it takes. They generally say that they work closely with their customers, but as you read their annual reports and examine the annual reports of competitors or customers, you will see the difference between those that do and those that do not. Look for companies where R&D has become a collaborative effort with prototypes, refinements, and tailor-made products. Such companies innovate around the needs of their customers.

It is critical to scrutinize whether management's claims about themselves align with what their customers think of them. Inability to understand how customers experience its products almost guarantees an eventual disconnect between the problems a business tries to solve and those customers need solving.

If the development process takes place in close co-operation with paying customers, the stock is scored one point.

## 6. Is constant heavy spending on marketing required for growth?

*Why does it matter?*

A lot of products rely on heavy marketing to maintain their market share. If the growth is not organic but pulled in by heavy marketing, it is easy to be misled into thinking that the product is great, when in fact it's just mediocre.

Yet, most companies use heavy marketing at the initial stage of the product life cycle to get customers. But abuse of this could be misleading. Once the initial hype is over, people might realize that they don't need the product. This is usually the case when a strategy is based on a specific product rather than a real need.

Amazon's founder Jeff Bezos once said; "More and more money will go into making a great customer experience, and less will go into shouting about the service. Word of mouth is becoming more powerful. If you offer a great service, people find out."

*How to assess it?*

The only way to tell if it is a genuinely great product, is to create growth that is more based on recommendations and word of mouth. The latter often means that customers ask for the company's products by brand name. Try to think of it in terms of how easy it is to acquire, and on-board new customers (i.e. the user acquisition cost).

If a sales success depends on continuous heavy marketing to maintain their market share, not just to encourage first timers to consume, this check is flagged.

This factor has a zero-weight impact on the scoring model for Business and is included as additional information to assist with investment decision-making.

# COMPETITIVE MOAT ANALYSIS

IS THIS A DEFENSIBLE BUSINESS
THAT CAN STAY COMPETITIVE?

Companies are born with potential to be great. But we cannot know how they will do until they are tested. Yet, profits attract competitors, and competition makes it difficult for companies to generate strong growth and margins over the long term.

In the end, defensibility is what will define the success of the business and make it attractive. Though, many investors are easily misled into focusing only on the rate of growth instead of trying to evaluate whether the business can earn excess returns in the long run – the longevity of growth. A company without defensibility is basically producing a commodity and typically has little to compete on besides price.

The best businesses are protected by some sort of durable competitive advantage that gives them longer-term viability of the business. Such companies can charge much more for its products than it costs to produce them, and can do it for many, many years. They do something special that is not easily replicable by competitors, as competitors eventually erode such advantages. Simply put, businesses with durable competitive advantages have built-in shock absorbers. All moats disappear over time, but great businesses have the longest shelf life.

Durable competitive advantages, also called competitive moats, are typically other than expensive capital, superior technology, specialised knowledge required to start up a similar business or being the first to start doing business in a new market, as they all tend to be temporary. Such advantages can begin to look like monopolies and yield huge but short-term profits before the competition has caught up. Similarly, higher profitability that comes from lower costs and product improvements will not lead to sustainable value creation without durable competitive advantages.

## WHAT DOES RETURN ON INVESTED CAPITAL MEAN?

Return on invested capital (ROIC) measures the return that an investment generates for those who have provided capital and how well a company generates cash flow relative to the capital it has invested in its core business. A high ROIC is generated by a combination of recurring revenues, high gross margins and low capital intensity. As such, ROIC is a proxy for the rate of compounding you could expect if a company were to retain its earnings, and reinvest, rather than paying them out as dividends.

> *Return on invested capital is calculated as:*
> *Return on Invested Capital (ROIC) = Net Operating Profit after Taxes / Invested Capital*

Where:

*Net Operating Profit after Taxes (NOPAT) = Operating Profit x (1 - Tax Rate)*

*Invested Capital (IC)* [1] *= Fixed Assets + Non-Cash Working Capital*

*Non-Cash Working Capital = Current Assets − Current Liabilities − Cash − Cash Equivalents*

[1] It should be noted that this formula excludes goodwill and intangible assets as they are unrelated to the economics of the core business. That doesn't mean that how much a company paid for past acquisitions doesn't matter, just that it is not relevant to the calculation of the underlying business's ROIC.

## COMPETITIVE MOAT CHECKLIST

1. Does the company enjoy market leadership?
2. Is the company's competitive position strengthening?
3. Do the company's returns on capital consistently exceed its cost of capital?
4. Does the business have a competitive moat that is easy to identify?
5. Does the company possess the ability to raise prices without losing customers?
6. *Has the gross profit margin declined over the past three years?*

∼

**1. Does the company enjoy market leadership?**

*Why does it matter?*

This check indicates whether the company enjoys market leadership as it highlights its ability to protect its turf - something that will have a direct impact on its ability to grow and flourish.

Market leadership puts the business in a strong position, allowing it to drive the market and create barriers to entry or scale for potential competitors. Also, competitors tend to focus on fighting weaker competitors while leaving the stronger ones alone.

*How to assess it?*

We consider a company a market leader if it is positioned to capture the greatest value in a growing market. It is not necessarily the largest player by market share, but rather the one that consistently outgrows its competitors and generates higher operating margins than them.

A niche market strategy typically means focusing on overlooked customer segments that high-cost incumbents are unwilling, or unable, to focus on. Yet, most great companies tend to start out focused on market leadership in a niche market and don't have the global leadership ambitions.

If the company is in the top three in a global market, or number one if it is a local operation or a small market niche, the stock is scored one point. If the company has no product sales yet, it scores no points.

## 2. Is the company's competitive position strengthening?

*Why does it matter?*

This check indicates whether the company is expected to have a growing market share for several years. If the customers are happy with the company's offering, it will be reflected in the market share. The bottom line is that a true moat doesn't just retain and maintain its existing customer base. It also attracts additional customers.

The greatest gains in a stock are usually made as a business is developing its competitive advantage rather than after it already has developed one. This is typically manifested in a growing market share. Whereas a declining market share indicates the opposite – problems with the product offering, customer dissatisfaction, and distribution challenges.

A business that is experiencing declining share is failing to attract new customers. Over time, it will lose its competitive advantage as existing customers either end up switching to other products or just quit buying them.

*How to assess it?*

We consider it as positive if the company is set to grow its market share over the next five years – or at least retain its market share if it is a market leader. What we are looking for here is a proven ability to win market share.

A good proxy for market share growth is increasing acceptance and usage of the company's product. This manifests itself in an increasing number of customers.

On the negative side, market share weakens if the threat of competition increases. The latter could be due to a shift in consumer demand based on patent expiration, a new disruptive technology or business model.

By comparing the ROIC growth rate in absolute terms and

relative to the growth experienced by its nearest competitor, we can better understand whether the company's competitive position is strengthening or weakening.

If the business is set to grow market share over the next five years, or at least retain its share if it is a market leader, the stock is scored one point. If the company has no product sales yet, it scores no points.

## 3. Do the company's returns on capital consistently exceed its cost of capital?

*Why does it matter?*

The good quantitative evidence of a moat is its ability to generate returns on capital that is greater than its cost of capital, and a history of doing so over time. This is the only way that growth adds any economic value. There is simply no value created when return on capital is below opportunity cost. In other words, a company whose return on capital is significantly above its opportunity cost over time, has a moat – whether they know it or not.

*How to assess it?*

Mathematical formulas won't tell you how to get a moat, but they can help prove that you have one. Look for a return on invested capital (ROIC) that is higher than its weighted average cost of capital (WACC) over time. In this question we examine whether this 'spread' has endured over the past three years.

If return on invested capital (ROIC) is significantly higher than weighted average cost of capital (WACC) over the past three years, the stock is scored one point. If the company has no product sales yet, it scores no points.

## 4. Does the business have a competitive moat that is easy to identify?

*Why does it matter?*

If a company has some sort of moat that makes it resilient in the face of competition, the likelihood that it can sustain high returns over a long period is higher.

Many companies will have a few consecutive years where they hit the curve right and earn high returns on capital despite not having a durable moat. Accordingly, it is important that you can identify the moat before paying up for growth.

*How to assess it?*

What determines whether a company has a competitive moat is both quantitative and qualitative. This check serves to validate the qualitative side by trying to identify elements that makes competition nearly impossible for competitors – factors that can hardly be copied, even with deep pockets. If you find these, the company probably has a strong competitive moat.

A good question to start with is: "What features are common to the longest lasting businesses within this sector?" This question will help you to understand what moat sources exist and are most relevant in a certain sector.

There are only a handful of competitive advantages that we consider real and sustainable barriers to entry, or moats. The primarily qualitative sources of moats are: (a) Scale Economies, (b) Special Assets, (c) Process Power, (d) Switching Costs, (e) Network Effects and (f) Brand Loyalty.

Finally, keep in mind that not all moats are global. They may only constitute a local structural competitive advantage.

For more about moats, see "Proxy Guide: Competitive Moats" on page 199.

If the business has a sustainable competitive advantage that is easy to identify and protects at least 50% of future earnings, the stock is scored one point.

## 5. Does the company possess the ability to raise prices without losing customers?

*Why does it matter?*

The existence of a sustainable competitive advantage, or moat, will typically be demonstrated by a company's pricing power, or consumer willingness to pay. This is the company's ability to set its own prices, rather than have the market dictate the prices. The latter means that the price for the product is negotiated and the company must lower the price to keep the customer.

The legendary Silicon Valley investor Marc Andreessen once said, "Raising prices is a great way to flesh out whether you actually have a moat. If you do have a moat, the customers will still buy... The definition of a moat is the ability to charge more."

Pricing power is the opportunity to raise prices in excess of inflation without fear of losing customers or being undercut by competitors. This means that a business can raise prices in real terms without affecting unit volume, to generate superior returns on capital. Nonetheless, it is not an unlimited or unchecked ability to raise prices at any rate the business desires.

Strong brands are a well-known source of pricing power. Pharmaceuticals are another notable example of pricing power, at least until patents expire.

*How to assess it?*

When assessing pricing power, gross profit margin growth and consistently high gross profit margins relative to industry peers tend to indicate pricing power, while volatility in these metrics suggests otherwise. However, don't rely too much on gross profits alone when comparing peers, as different companies account for expenses differently.

Michael Shearn, who is the author of *The Investment Checklist*, highlights several key characteristics in pricing power:

1. Companies that have high customer retention rates;
2. Customers who have low price sensitivity or only spend a small percentage of their budget on the business's product;
3. Customers that have plenty of cash or highly profitable business models;
4. Customers where the quality of the product is more important than the price and a higher price is signalling higher quality.

Also, pay close attention when you see competitive industries undergoing rationalisations. As soon as they are consolidated down to three players (creating an oligopoly), the pain may already be gone and rational pricing will typically follow. Consolidated industries generally create a sort of pent-up pricing power that can be released in the form of real price increases. The message here is that you may find real pricing power in businesses that for some reason have not raised prices for a long period of time.

Finally, to sustain pricing power, the company needs to constantly improve the value it offers to the customer. If it doesn't, its customers may become reluctant to accept the price or product innovation, allowing competitors to overtake or disrupt them. However, if the company remains at the forefront of innovation, it should be able to increase prices in line with the added customer benefits the innovation generates. Hence, when you look at pricing power you should always look at the company's growth strategy, particularly if it keeps investing in its moat sources.

For more about moats, see "Proxy Guide: Competitive Moats" on page 199.

If the company has sustainable pricing power to increase prices above inflation without hurting unit volume, then the stock is scored one point. If the company has no product sales yet, it scores no points.

**6 . *Has the gross profit margin declined over the past three years?***

*Why does it matter?*

A declining gross margin is a warning sign. If competition gets tough or a company loses its competitive advantage, its gross margin usually declines. When revenues drop and the cost of making the goods stays the same, the gross margin will decline.

Conversely, gross margin growth over time is a good indicator of a company's ability to reduce costs or maintain price increases without losing customers, i.e. achieving cost efficiency and/or pricing power.

*How to assess it?*

If the gross profit margin is lower than three years ago, this check is flagged.

This factor has a zero-weight impact on the scoring model for Business and is included as additional information to assist with investment decision-making.

# PROXY GUIDE: COMPETITIVE MOATS

Competitive moats are a business' capacity to maintain competitive advantages that preserve its long-term profitability and market share in the face of competition. Companies with competitive moats typically survive financially even if management talent does not deliver as expected or if they leave the business. Finding companies with genuine moats is not easy. It takes time and research. However, an extensive literature has emerged since Warren Buffett first introduced the concept.

We divide all moats on the basis of price or cost advantages - the two main factors that define a company's profitability. Below six common competitive moats are described briefly:

**Cost Advantages**

Companies that enjoy cost structure advantages produce better quality at a lower price than the competition or just apply price pressure to knock them out. This involves creating a product much cheaper, both to make and supply.

SCALE ECONOMIES: Generate economies of scale in production (buying power) and large distribution networks, as per-unit costs fall with increasing output, creating a 'flywheel' that accelerates as the business grows. For example, building software costs the same regardless of the number of people buying it. Relative size matters more than absolute size as it makes the cost of gaining share prohibitive. Even so, economies of scale tend to dissipate when the market gets large enough.

SPECIAL ASSETS: Benefit from privileged access at attractive terms to certain assets or resources that can independently enhance value like patents, ownership, licenses, government approvals, proprietary technology, superior business model, strong distribution network, or location/geographical proximity, as in cases like airports and mines. These are all elements that competitors cannot access or match without suffering a net economic loss.

For example, if a company has a strong distribution network that reaches its customers effectively and efficiently, it has a huge advantage over other competitors that lack such distribution. Also, a company with a strong distribution moat will also be able to enter new areas to expand its total addressable market (TAM) as its competitive advantage does not depend on a specific product, but rather its ability to distribute any relevant product. Such companies typically leverage their strong distribution moats by distributing acquired products to a wider audience than what the originator companies could access themselves.

Peter Thiel, puts this point well in his great book *Zero to One*: "Superior sales and distribution by itself can create a monopoly, even with no product differentiation. The converse is not true."

PROCESS POWER: Depend on a series of chain-linked core activities to provide a whole product, which rivals cannot readily replicate or do by hiring away the people. To gain success with process power each core activity must be performed well, as they reinforce each other. Still, it takes significant trial and error to get the needed reinforcing actions in place – to make them deeply embedded inside the organisation.

**Price Advantages**

Companies that enjoy price advantages lock out competitors through high entry and scalability barriers to sustainably earn high profit margins. This involves creating a product that is convenient, emotionally appealing, and very easy to use – or simply high quality.

SWITCHING COSTS: Make it cost more for customers to switch to an alternative supplier than to remain. This means that first-mover companies have the potential to enjoy high switching costs if they scale fast. Still, this value can only be captured if a buyer purchases repeatedly or buys add-on products. Note that switching costs come in many forms– money, time, risk and inconvenience (breaking good business relationships, for example).

Sometimes, the competitive advantage of a business is a result of very long product lifecycles associated with inability to exit from the initial investment leading to relatively insurmountable switching costs. Typically, this happens when a business can embed itself in the customer's business processes in a way that it becomes prohibitive for the customer to switch. In such cases, if the supplier can generate substantial aftermarket revenues, it will have endowed itself with a substantial competitive advantage.

NETWORK EFFECTS: Provide a product where every new user makes the product more valuable to all other users. This is like scale economies, but instead of reducing the producer's cost it increases the buyer's willingness to pay. To be able to scale fast it's critical to get the product right early on, as networks win only at scale and have a 'winner takes it all' boundedness.

For example, in a two-sided network like an auction or a marketplace business, more buyers showing up will attract more sellers, and that in turn will attract more buyers. Once this positive cycle is in place, it becomes nearly impossible to convince either buyer or seller to leave and join a new platform. Businesses such as eBay and Airbnb have built up strong two-sided networks over time.

Different types of network effects are stronger or weaker than others, and they each work differently– learn more about them at www.nfx.com.

BRAND LOYALTY: Create a strong brand that will earn superior returns to those with no branding. A strong brand means consistency and a promise to consumers, who will prefer it over any other, almost regardless of price or convenience and sometimes even if the product is substandard. Loyal customers are simply less tempted by other offers and incentives since it is the label, not the product, that bestows brand loyalty.

Brands can create customer loyalty through one or both of these two routes:

- Reducing uncertainty as the customer attains 'peace of mind', knowing that the product will be as just as expected. This happens through (a) lower search costs as an informational advantage of being well-known and/or (b) good reputation to confer legitimacy.

- Eliciting good feelings about the product, distinct from the objective value. This happens when it signals status to express individuality.

However, creating a strong brand typically takes a long investment runway with no assurance of success. Also, counterfeiters with inconsistent offerings may undermine it. Efforts to copy another brand run the risk of trademark infringement actions with their related costs and uncertain outcomes. Finally, branding is a non-exclusive advantage, which means that a competitor can target the same customers with an equally impactful brand (Prada, Louis Vuitton and Hermès, for example).

# OPERATIONAL RISK ANALYSIS

## DOES THE BUSINESS HAVE LIMITED EXPOSURE TO SIGNIFICANT OPERATIONAL RISKS?

All investment evaluations should start by measuring risk. Negative events, speed bumps, and glancing blows will occur even during the maturation of great companies. It's your job to know the difference between a glancing blow and a knockout punch that could sink the business.

At the extreme are those businesses whose revenues depend on binary outcomes where either the company achieves major success or perishes completely (biotech and e-commerce companies are examples). This is typically the case for companies where revenues come from a single product or title as these are typically one-time in nature.

Likewise, the risk is high when revenues are tied to commodity prices (such as oil and gas companies) or when the businesses rely on a small number of large one-off contracts. The latter means the businesses could see earnings take a sharp downward turn if one contract is cancelled or, even worse, if future contracts become scarce.

In such businesses you're basically always operating in the dark and are restricted in making realistic forecasts. Understanding such risks are very important since growth and profitability could be highly unstable. That's why you need to evaluate the operational risks to avoid being overly confident of a company's future prospects.

## OPERATIONAL RISK CHECKLIST

1. Does the business have a wide revenue base?
2. Are the business's earnings largely unaffected by commodity prices?
3. Is the business relatively immune to regulatory risk?
4. Is the business independent of any major partners?
5. Is the business defensive and independent of market conditions?
6. *Does the business depend on key employees for its future success?*

∽

### 1. Does the business have a wide revenue base?

*Why does it matter?*

The ideal situation is a diversified customer base and wide geographic distribution, with multiple sources of revenue where each product contributes significantly to profits. In other words, you want to avoid companies that sell only one product to one group of customers in one market.

A high dependence on a product or a small number of customers could lead to two potential disasters. If the product goes away or is made obsolete, or the customers find a new supplier, it will leave a significant dent in the company's revenue.

Likewise, if the customer doesn't leave but has significant bargaining power, it can reduce the company's revenue. Customers that represent a large percentage of the revenue simply have 'bargain power' that is likely to result in pricing, feature, or service demands over time. That's why companies with excessive customer concentration will generally attract a lower valuation multiple.

Moreover, although countries' economies and markets have become more connected, it does not follow that they are all in sync with each other. At any time some may be experiencing strong growth while others are mired in recession.

*How to assess it?*

To determine whether a company has a wide revenue base, the following three criteria are evaluated:

1. No single customer accounts for more than 10% of sales
2. No single product accounts for more than 20% of sales
3. No single country accounts for more than 60% of sales

If all three criteria are fulfilled, the stock is scored one point.

## 2. Are the business's earnings largely unaffected by commodity prices?

*Why does it matter?*

Commodity prices are volatile and highly unpredictable. As a result, investing in companies where the revenues are tied to commodity prices is gambling to an extent, as they are at the mercy of the market. They are price takers. The company's revenues, profits and stocks will rise and fall in volatile fashion with the price of the commodity. No one is able to accurately forecast the price of commodities over time.

This is why we find that most executive teams in these types of companies behave in a pro-cyclical fashion. In other words, they take a lot of risk at the top of the cycle and are forced to make the wrong decisions at the bottom of the cycle by raising new capital, etc.

*How to assess it?*

If the company's earnings aren't tied to commodity prices to a large extent, the company's income is considered to be independent of commodity price changes.

If the company's earnings are largely unaffected by commodity prices, the stock is scored one point.

### 3. Is the business relatively immune to regulatory risk?

*Why does it matter?*

Unexpected regulatory changes can send shockwaves around the markets and destroy companies. Accordingly, it's a good idea to spend some time thinking about the regulatory risks that a company is exposed to. Given the arbitrary nature of many political decisions, even the most expert analysts struggle to predict how a government's actions might impact a particular stock.

Some companies receive their revenue from government sources, either directly or indirectly. But if the government is able to change the amount of revenue received due to budget changes, for example, the earnings of these companies whose products are subsidised by the government will always be at risk. A reduction in this subsidy would increase the cost for consumers and subsequently reduce the demand.

Likewise, businesses regulated by the government are at risk of a change in laws and regulations, as these can have a deep impact on pricing and operating costs or change the competitive landscape. That's usually the case for pharma companies, for example, given the importance of regulatory agencies in approving and reimbursing new drugs.

Always factor in a high likelihood of negative aggressive regulation of business models that the government doesn't approve of, like gambling or consumer loans. Corporate executives typically ignore these sorts of developments because it is just more convenient not to take in information that things might be changing. Yet it's entirely possible for companies to cease operations as a consequence of new regulations.

*How to assess it?*

If the company's revenues aren't heavily regulated or at risk of being targeted by regulation at some point in the future, they are considered independent of regulations.

If the business is relatively immune to regulatory risk, the stock is scored one point.

## 4. Is the business independent of any major partners?

*Why does it matter?*

No one likes to be at the mercy of a partner. Investors will discount the valuation of any company that is heavily dependent on another partner today or in the future in some way. Suppliers may have a duopoly, which weakens the company's ability to negotiate favourable purchase agreements. This is typically the case when the company rely on a highly concentrated supplier base with little to no competition.

The bottom line is that strong dependencies eat away at investors simply because the company is exposed to issues that are out of the control of management. And even if the partner doesn't impact them, the mere awareness that they could, can have a dramatic impact on long-term valuation.

*How to assess it?*

If no single partner accounts for more than 20% of sales, the company is considered to not be highly dependent on any major partner. This includes any large license, contract, or patent expiry.

If the business is independent of any major partners, the stock is scored one point.

## 5. Is the business defensive and independent of market conditions?

*Why does it matter?*

An industry may be in a strong growth period and look very attractive, but it may also be at the peak of a cycle that is possibly about to turn substantially negative. A cyclical business will report the highest earnings at the top of a cycle, right before income is about to decline. Investors often fall for cyclical stocks exactly when their valuations start to imply strong growth far into the future.

People love extrapolation and forget that cycles exist. Yet, many companies follow the cycle of the economy, meaning that their performance will be cyclical and relatively unpredictable. When expansionary periods are sustained for surprisingly long time, people begin to believe that cyclicality has been conquered, and growth starts to look sustainable when it is not.

The best companies are those that do well when the economy is doing well and don't miss a beat when the economy falls into recession. Demand for their products is stable rather than cyclical, which contributes to steady top-line growth. As a result, companies that sell necessities, rather than products that are merely desired, are likely to do better in a recession. In other words, defensive stocks hold up much better than cyclical ones in market crises and recessions – or at least rebound faster.

*How to assess it?*

If the business isn't cyclically fragile and can grow despite the overall economy, the company's revenues are considered recession-proof to a high degree. Such companies typically sell products that are necessities that address a very basic need for their customers. Instead, cyclical stocks are those that correlate with the overall economy, including luxury items and other discretionary spending. Try to understand how the last recession hit the company. Also consider the extent to which its products are exposed to the cyclicality of its customers' markets.

Likewise, companies that depend on access to capital markets to raise cash are indirectly dependent on the overall economy to grow their business. Accordingly, companies that are highly dependent on market conditions should be considered cyclical.

If the business is neither in a market with cyclical demand nor is dependent on the capital markets, the stock is scored one point.

NOTE: Companies that operate in defensive markets are not necessarily better investments than companies that operate in cyclical markets, but at least management doesn't have to deal with the business cycle on top of everything else.

The key to successful investing in cyclical companies is to look for companies that are able to operate at low prices and with little debt. If not, the company may not make it out to the other side of the cycle.

This dictates that the company must have the ability to counteract lower revenues by lowering costs.

## 6. *Does the business depend on key employees for its future success?*

*Why does it matter?*

Companies with key employees are typically small businesses that depend heavily on just a handful of people who are essential to its business. What happens if a key employee leaves, becomes ill or dies? If this has an outsized impact on the company's overall health, it is a considerable operational risk. This is certainly the case with founder-led companies.

Likewise, employees in many service companies are effectively in control of their own business, without necessarily being shareholders. Such service companies may earn high returns on capital, but only because capital isn't needed. This is typically the case for investment banks, law firms, fund managers, consultancy companies, and head-hunters. Despite supposedly high returns on capital in these businesses, the value creation may mostly benefit key employees. As a result, the opportunities to earn attractive returns in such companies are typically rather limited for external shareholders as the company is probably being run for the benefit of management and key employees.

*How to assess it?*

Ask yourself if the business model depends on execution and requires considerable faith in key employees or is being run for insiders. If the answer is 'Yes', this check is flagged.

Likewise, the check is flagged when the growth stalls because key employees aren't able to do what's right for the company and its investors.

This factor has a zero-weight impact on the scoring model for Business and is included as additional information to assist with investment decision-making.

# SOCIAL RESPONSIBILITY ANALYSIS
DOES THE BUSINESS OPERATE IN A SOCIALLY AND ENVIRONMENTALLY RESPONSIBLE WAY?

Sustainable profitability can only be achieved by treating stakeholders fairly. In the same manner that Buffett views reputation as a bottom line worthy of care equal to the profit margin, so too is social wellbeing of all stakeholders. According to this type of holistic thinking, responsible businesses ought to track their 'triple bottom line' – their economic, sociocultural, and environmental performance – and in this way gain a sustained competitive advantage for their business.

Environmental and social issues are hard to pin-point but do ultimately impact the long-term health of a business. In short, they require viewing treatment of workers, communities and the environment as equal in importance to profit-making. They are about making products people need and doing so without hurting the planet.

A sustainable corporate culture is critical to competitive capacity. A business can benefit from pursuing sustainable development in two basic ways – by driving cost efficiencies and by generating top-line growth. Cost savings can come from better operational performance, improved recruitment and retention of talented employees, and lower business risk and improved safety. Increased revenue can come from learning and innovation, enhanced recognition and reputation, better customer loyalty, improved supply chain management and access to capital.

The bottom line is that socially responsible investing improves returns and those who don't factor sustainability in will be at a disadvantage.

## SOCIAL RESPONSIBILITY CHECKLIST

1. Are the products for the greater good?
2. Has the company avoided sustainability-related incidents over the past five years?
3. Does the company have a purpose-driven leadership?
4. Do employees enjoy working for the company?
5. Are sustainability indicators incorporated into the incentive system?
6. *Does the company lack disclosure on environmental and social issues?*

**1. Are the products for the greater good?**

*Why does it matter?*

Many investors only want to invest in companies that operate responsibly and have a positive impact on the world. These are not usually involved in tobacco, alcohol, pornography, gambling, weaponry, abuse of human rights or environmental negatives like air and water pollution (fossil fuel companies, for example). The rationale is that if the product is for the greater good it is a net benefit to society that the company exists.

The greater good implies that companies contribute to a more circular economy. They reduce environmental impact by more sustainable use of natural resources and a more responsible consumption or utilisation of assets. Leaving behind the old 'take, make & waste' model, the new frontier is re-design, re-use & repair to avoid unnecessary waste.

Circular business models include opportunities for less volatile input costs that lead to higher margins. This could involve remanufacturing of a product into the same condition as a new product or production methods with lower dependence on raw materials. It may also feature better efficiency and working capital management by changing the ownership concept from property to sharing.

*How to assess it?*

Try to assess whether the company recognises revenue in an ethical and responsible manner. You need to think of not just what it does but how it does it and what it uses. Sometimes an apparent failure on the 'greater good' question is not necessarily the full story.

For example, a company that makes submarines - weapons that can cause mass destruction - also helps keep the peace. A second take reveals a company that contributes to a more secure world in which these products are used properly.

If the company's products make a positive impact on the world, the stock is scored one point.

## 2. Has the company avoided sustainability-related incidents over the past five years?

*Why does it matter?*

Today even the most socially and environmentally responsible brands can find themselves on the receiving end of heated activist campaigns. While isolated and smaller sustainability-related (environmental or ethical) issues might not derail a business, repeated incidents or a major one can tarnish a corporate reputation, diminish trust and make a company more vulnerable to problems in the future.

*How to assess it?*

Sustainability-related incidents are any major environmental or ethical issues that could result in penalties or negative publicity with a significant long-term business impact on the company. Google phrases like '<Company name> crisis OR litigation' and you will find opinion pieces.

If the company has faced no major environmental or ethical issues or litigations over the last five years, the stock is scored one point.

### 3. Does the company have a purpose-driven leadership?

*Why does it matter?*

Whatever drives us, we all derive happiness from finding purpose. A corporate purpose is an expression of the change the company wants to bring about in the world, as well as a unique approach or 'way' that will bring it about.

Purpose is a key element for any company to stay relevant in a fast-changing world. It represents something more than profits that should guide the company's operations – a 'north star' to follow in all major decisions. It is also something that helps employees feel more personally committed to the business.

The best performing businesses over the long term, as measured by shareholder returns, are very often purpose-driven. Their CEOs use purpose to generate sustained profitable growth, stay relevant in a rapidly changing world and deepen ties with their stakeholders as purpose creates a sense of community. Companies that survive are in essence communities that customers, employees and owners want to be a part of.

A strong purpose help CEOs redefine their market as they look for opportunities in the larger ecosystem rather than feeling limited to their current playing field. Also, it allows them to reshape their value propositions by responding to trends, building on trust, and focusing on customer pain points. This in turn enables them to overcome the challenges of slowing growth and declining profitability.

*How to assess it?*

Purpose can be quite difficult to evaluate since even the worst companies will have some sort of generic mission statement that they pretend to believe in. Yet most companies were started because the founders were passionate about solving a problem – idealists whose vision was about making the world better in some way – not because they wanted to become wealthy.

Look for companies whose managers and employees are passionate about the company's mission and want to do right by their stakeholders. Ask managers why they do what they do, what are their moral boundaries, why do they exist beyond financial gain? Do their employees have that sense of purpose, why do they come to work every day?

This reason for existing isn't meant to be a strategic differentiator, but an aspirational goal that drives the organisation. A good purpose should capture what a company aspires to be and do. It is an ambition, a cause, something which the company and its customers can strive for together, and something that makes the world a better place. Most importantly, it has to be believed by most people in the organisation.

Many companies consider purpose merely an add-on to their strategy, but a truly purpose-driven company puts it at its core. To determine whether a company has properly translated its purpose into action, management need to answer 'yes' to all of the following questions:

1) Does purpose contribute to increasing your company's growth and profitability today?

2) Does purpose significantly influence your strategic decisions and investment choices?

3) Does purpose shape your core value proposition?

4) Does purpose affect how you build and manage your organisational capabilities?

5) Is purpose on the agenda of your leadership team every time you meet?

Additionally, a company genuinely delivering on its purpose will typically have a passionate and loyal fan base.

Even if this is a check-the-box exercise with management, you should verify it by doing some background work with employees outside the management team. See 'How to Conduct Your Channel Checks' on page 349.

If the company has a well-defined purpose and management answers yes to all five questions above, the stock is scored one point.

## 4. Do employees enjoy working for the company?

*Why does it matter?*

Attracting and retaining talent is the most tangible benefits of a positive work environment. After all, one of the limiting factors for many companies is access to talent. Particularly in industries where the quality of ideas dictates success, the ability to attract talent should not be underestimated. Most talented employees will gladly sacrifice pay for the right work environment. When the employees of a business are excited to show up to work regardless of compensation, that's when magic starts to happen.

If people are happy and feel good about coming to work, they work more productively and tend to stay with a company much longer than unfulfilled employees. Long-term employees provide better customer service due to their greater experience and knowledge. And when customers receive more knowledgeable service, they have a better experience and are more likely to do business with the company again. Also, they are less price-sensitive and generate positive word-of-mouth.

The bottom line is that happy employees lead to happy customers, and happy customers ensure that shareholders are happy too. Employees with positive attitudes towards their work carry this over to customers and strive to deliver high-quality service, resulting in increased customer happiness and loyalty. Moreover, employees who are happy and committed to their workplace genuinely want to see the company do well. They are a vital asset in maintaining a strong reputation, brand image and competitive advantage. However, all other things being equal, employees at strongly performing companies will always be more satisfied.

*How to assess it?*

Try to talk to some of the employees directly and visiting the headquarters. It should be quite clear if employees enjoy working for the company. Look for a collegial and family-oriented environment where best practices are shared and people are driven by the same overall desire to succeed. In such a collaborative culture, employees don't fear political retaliation or tolerate verbal abuse (usually by 'high-performance' employees), both common signs of a broken culture.

These are typically companies that focus on performance indicators and where decisions are made as close to the customer as possible in a decentralised, non-bureaucratic process. Decentralised companies often have limited staff functions and organise themselves into small, tight, agile teams with considerable autonomy and earned trust. Business unit managers are typically given much control over their activities, while pay is based on merit and performance. Likewise, managers who pay attention to vision, strategies, culture and inspiration are often promoted, rather than skilled mangers who are not necessarily leaders. This in turn incentivises entrepreneurship and makes employees more likely to take responsibility.

Consequently, be very cautious towards arrogant, imperial CEOs who centralize power around themselves. These CEOs tend to have very little room for critique and if someone try to do anything innovative, they are likely to be reprimanded. 'My way or the highway' leadership styles don't play well in today's world and will often result in a fractured culture – and ultimately a non-productive organisation. People don't want to be micro-managed and monitored every moment of every day. Nonetheless, such organisations exist where no one is trusted to do their job.

How senior managers treat their employees is a good clue as to how they will treat their shareholders. Sir Richard Branson says, "Train people well enough so they can leave. Treat them well enough so they don't want to." Management investing significant resources in employee training and contributing to employees' well-being is a great sign. Higher employee engagement typically follows when management promotes health and happiness through investment in employee wellness programs, office architecture, furnishings and high-end technology and other corporate perks. These are all worthwhile for frugal organisations that value long-term outcomes, as opposed to cheap managements that focus on minimising costs.

A good complementary sign is if the company's employee turnover rate is low compared to its closest competitors. Similarly, a low level of sick leave among employees is a good sign. Looking at average salaries, employee shareholdings and bonus plans can also give sense of how involved employees are – particularly at professional services and similar companies.

Another way to get a sense of employee happiness is to read reviews on Glassdoor.com. Although some are clearly fake, the site gives decent insight into employee sentiment at companies. Likewise, a review of Twitter and LinkedIn for people who work at the company may offer some unusual insights.

If employees enjoy working for the company, the stock is scored one point.

## 5. Are sustainability indicators incorporated into the incentive system?

*Why does it matter?*

The purpose of a company is not just to produce profits, it is to produce solutions to problems of people and planet and in the process to produce profits. That is why incentive plans should reward positive environmental or social impact alongside financial returns.

Never underestimate the power of incentives. Incorporating sustainability considerations into the incentive system will highlight the integration of sustainability in daily work as a way of encouraging managers and employees to take a long-term view for sustainable value creation. This especially includes being proactive in identifying and acting on unethical behaviour that could damage the company's reputation.

It is important that success metrics are tangible, challenging yet achievable, and well communicated. Equally, performance targets need to align clearly with reality and benefit all parties involved to ensure strong performance over the long term. Accordingly, companies should explain and justify their pay arrangements in a meaningful way that is specific to the business and its strategy rather than through boilerplate generic statements.

*How to assess it?*

The right incentive system is key to driving results. This means that senior executives' compensation must be linked to the company's performance on environmental and social metrics. Look for remuneration and incentive structures that reward people for working toward sustainable value creation. Keep in mind that incentive plans are not just about paying more money for better results – they also can encourage managers to make the right choices that support the strategy and overall mission (the answer to the question, "Why do we exist and what do we contribute?").

A well-designed employee reward program is not about paying more to get better results. It's about getting employees personally motivated to meet company targets, track KPIs that are impacted by their performance, and keep outperforming and prioritising sustainable returns.

However, make sure that compensation is based on multiple metrics rather than just one. No single metric can perfectly capture an underlying strategy as no single number tells the whole story. Moreover, employees are far less likely to substitute a performance metric for the strategy itself when they have to meet targets on multiple metrics.

Below are seven criteria listed that promote corporate sustainability:

1. Incentive plan that supports the strategic plan
2. Clear correlation between company performance and payouts, i.e. tracking multiple Key Performance Indicators (KPIs) that impact compensation
3. Certain sustainability standards* need to have been met before payout, even if all financial targets have been met, e.g. customer satisfaction or reduction in use of more hazardous chemicals
4. Clawback provision for executive compensation where outstanding long-term incentive awards are forfeited in the event of termination for cause
5. Variable compensation spending is directly tied to company affordability metrics
6. No acceleration of long-term award vesting upon retirement or any other form of termination
7. Rewards are tied to multiyear business goals, that can be valued annually based on objective performance metrics.

If incentive schemes check all seven sustainability criteria, the stock is scored one point.

* As with all performance measures these should be material to the business, clear and transparent with specified metrics and targets that are measurable.

## 6. Does the company lack disclosure on key environmental and social issues?

*Why does it matter?*

Stakeholders increasingly demand that businesses create value for, and not simply extract value from, the communities in which they operate. Being a good corporate steward simply means going beyond having a community investment program or using recycled paper. Today climate change, human rights legislation, gender pay equality, and marketing practices are just some of the potential risk factors requiring disclosure by companies.

Most companies acknowledge in their reports the importance of environmental and social issues, but more often than not is this information not clear enough in terms of 'significant' environmental or social issues. Sustainability reporting should include clear metrics with a proper context. This will help investors to gauge success over time in meeting these goals.

*How to assess it?*

The key is to assess whether the company discloses its exposure to and management of significant environmental and social issues that might impact its valuation. A company that spends vast sums of money trying to address every conceivable issue is likely to see its financial performance suffer. Distinguishing between materiality and what's significant from a social point of view is key to effective sustainability reporting.

For example, greenhouse gas emissions are significant for an electric utility company but less so for a financial services company. Similarly, supply chain management is more significant for an apparel company using low-cost workers in developing countries than for a pharmaceutical company.

If the company lacks disclosure on its exposure to and management of key environmental and social risks, the check is flagged.

This factor has a zero-weight impact on the scoring model for Business and is included as additional information to assist with investment decision-making.

# FINANCIAL TENETS

## DOES THE BUSINESS HAVE SOLID FINANCIAL FUNDAMENTALS?

# BACKGROUND

Investing is part art, part science. Financial ratios make up most of the science. Ratios are used to evaluate the financial soundness of a business. The analysis involves the calculation and comparison of ratios derived from a company's financial statements. These ratios are key factors that will impact a company's financial performance and valuation. However, you only need a few to determine whether a company is financially strong or weak.

While ratio analysis is extremely useful and necessary for your investing, it does have limitations. Financial ratios only look at past figures. As such, it is difficult to use them to forecast the future. However, ratios can give an indication of whether the trend is likely to persist or not and help you make better investment decisions. Even so, for companies with a short business history it becomes trickier to do any meaningful analysis. This is likely to lead to a lower score, indicating a higher risk – the purpose of the quality rating system.

## THE FRAMEWORK

The Financial rating is based on quantitative scores that are grouped into five separate categories: Earnings Power, Profit Margin, Growth Rate, Financial Health and Earnings Quality.

All of these sub-categories are assessed on five checks of quantitative and qualitative questions. Each check is allocated one point if the question can be answered with a 'Yes'; the total number of these points makes up each sub-category's score on a scale that ranges from 0 to 5 rounded to the nearest whole number. If unsure about a question or disclosure is inadequate, the check fails by default. This is consistent with the best ideas often being the simplest.

Each sub-category also includes a sixth complementary check. These negative questions provide additional information to assist with investment decision-making, but do not impact the scoring model.

# EARNINGS POWER ANALYSIS

## DOES THE COMPANY HAVE STRONG EARNINGS CAPACITY?

The earnings power of an investment should always be measured as terms of rate of return, not as absolute earnings or dividends. Earnings power reflects the ability of the stock to earn above-average rates of return at above-average growth rates. Return on Assets (ROA) and Return on Equity (ROE) are the two most prevalent metrics used to obtain an idea of the returns a company generates, and to compare this return generation to the company's peers. While important information about a company's profit-generating efficiency can be learned from each one of these two metrics, they will likely each follow a similar trajectory.

## What does Return on Assets mean?

Return on Assets (ROA) measures the productivity of the company's assets. Rather than measure Net Profit as a percentage of equity, it uses assets used in generating earnings for the company.

It is a broad measure of the efficiency of asset usage by the company and is often used to compare if a company is more or less effectively using its assets than its industrial peers.

We use earnings before taxes (EBT) to remove the impact of taxation, as companies operate in jurisdictions with different tax policies.

Return on Assets is calculated as:

$$Return\ on\ Assets\ (ROA) = Earnings\ Before\ Taxes\ /\ Average\ Total\ Assets$$

We use the average total assets for the period in question, since a company's total assets can vary over time depending on purchases, sales and seasonal fluctuations.

## What does Return on Equity mean?

Return on Equity (ROE) is the profit made as a percentage of shareholders' equity. It determines how efficient the company is at using both shareholder's capital and debt to produce income.

A higher ROE means a greater bang for every buck invested by shareholders, but also that there is less need to borrow or sell more shares to grow. The latter is because surplus funds can be invested to improve business operations.

If the Return on Equity is higher than the Return on Assets, the business is generating higher returns for its shareholders than it is paying in interest. In effect, it is successfully leveraging borrowed funds.

We use average shareholder equity to calculate ROE as shareholder equity in a company can fluctuate over the period during which the net income has been earned. For instance, dividends reduce shareholder equity and boost ROE, whereas a new share issue lowers ROE.

The beginning and end of the period should coincide with the period during which net income is earned.

Return on Equity is calculated as:

*Return on Equity = Net Profit / Average Shareholder Equity (Book Value)*

If shareholders' equity is negative, the most common issue is excessive debt or inconsistent profitability. However, there are exceptions to that rule for companies that are profitable and have been using cash flow to buy back their own shares. In all cases, negative or extremely high ROE levels should be considered a warning sign worth investigating.

## EARNINGS POWER CHECKLIST

1. Has Return on Assets (ROA) been consistently above the industry average?
2. Is Return on Equity (ROE) higher than 10%?
3. Has Return on Equity (ROE) increased over the past three years?
4. Is average Return on Equity (ROE) at least 20% for the past five years?
5. Has Return on Equity (ROE) been consistent over the past seven years?
6. *Does Return on Equity (ROE) appear unsustainably high?*

**1. Has Return on Assets (ROA) consistently been above the industry average?**

*Why does it matter?*

This check measures whether the company is better at using assets to generate profit than its competitors. The best companies do well consistently, showing discipline during boom years and taking advantage of opportunities during down years.

All other things being equal, capital-intensive companies where the business requires a large amount of capital to grow have lower ROA than companies with lower capital requirements. Unless such companies have a superior asset turnover, they are less interesting from the shareholder perspective because a larger portion of current cash flow is spent on maintenance investments – expenditures they have to make just to keep the lights on.

*How to assess it?*

If ROA is greater than the relevant industry average for every single year of the last five, the stock is scored one point.

## 2. Is Return on Equity (ROE) higher than 10%?

*Why does it matter?*

This check offers a gauge of a company's earnings potential. It indicates whether it's a profit machine or an inefficient clunker, as a company cannot grow earnings faster than its current ROE without raising additional funds.

Public companies have historically earned a ROE of 10% to 15% on average. Accordingly, a company that achieves returns on equity of less than 10% has poor earnings power.

*How to assess it?*

If ROE for the company for the last year is greater than 10%, the stock is scored one point.

## 3. Has Return on Equity (ROE) increased over the past three years?

*Why does it matter?*

This check measures a company's profitability trend as there is a strong correlation between the stock performance and profitability over the long-term. An improving ROE is a very good sign as it generally means that management has improved its ability to generate a profit. This is most likely because Net Profit has increased in relation to common equity, and a higher Net Profit is always a positive – all other things being equal.

*How to assess it?*

If the last year ROE is greater than 1x the ROE from three years ago, the stock is scored one point. If no operating profit has been reported in any of the last three years, or if the company has negative shareholders' equity, it scores no points.

## 4. Is average Return on Equity (ROE) at least 20% for the past five years?

*Why does it matter?*

This check offers a gauge of a company's earnings potential. It indicates whether it's a profit machine or an inefficient clunker, as a company cannot grow earnings faster than its current ROE without raising additional funds. It's generally accepted that a ROE of 20% or higher is indicative of a company which is highly efficient.

However, to grow at the current ROE assumes all profits are reinvested back into the business. Very few companies can sustain 100% reinvestment rates at high returns for very long periods of time.

*How to assess it?*

If the average ROE for the past five years is greater than 20%, the stock is scored one point. If no Net Profit has been reported in any of the last five years or if the company has negative shareholders' equity, it scores no points.

## 5. Has Return on Equity (ROE) been consistent over the past seven years?

*Why does it matter?*

This check measures if the company generates consistent and steady profits as it typically means increased predictability in future profitability. A company can fake good ROE for a couple of years. But to achieve high ROE for seven consecutive years is something else. Such a long time period will capture performance during different economic conditions and therefore can adequately measure consistency of results.

*How to assess it?*

If there have been no annual drops in ROE greater than 10% (the relative measure, not percentage points) in the past seven years, the stock is scored one point. If no Net Profit has been reported in any of the last seven years or the company has negative shareholders' equity, it scores no points.

## 6. Does Return on Equity (ROE) appear unsustainably high?

*Why does it matter?*

This check indicates if ROE is likely to be unsustainable over time due to the company's profitability, earnings stability and leverage. In short, ROE can be deceptive if viewed on its own. Indeed, what has mattered historically for market-beating share price performance is a company's ability to sustain a high ROE over time.

It turns out there are a few tell-tale signs of unsustainable ROE:

A) DECLINING PROFITABILITY

Non-financial companies:

*Has Operating Cash Flow to Operating Assets declined for three years in a row?*

Financial institutions:

*Has Net Interest Margin declined for three years in a row?*

B) HIGH VARIABILITY IN EARNINGS

All companies:

*Have there been annual drops in Net Profit of more than 20% in the past seven years?*

C) HIGH FINANCIAL LEVERAGE

Non-financial companies:

*Is the Debt to Equity ratio 50% or higher?*

Financial institutions:

*Is Assets to Equity ratio 15x or higher?*

If any of the three questions above is answered with a 'Yes', the company appears to have an unsustainable high ROE and this check is flagged.

This factor has a zero-weight impact on the scoring model for Financials and is included as additional information to assist with investment decision-making.

# PROFIT MARGINS ANALYSIS

HAS THE COMPANY GENERATED HIGH AND CONSISTENT PROFIT MARGINS?

When it comes to evaluating a company's financial performance, profit margin analysis is one of the key aspects in assessing success. An improvement in margins requires lower costs and/or higher prices for the company's product. Steady growth in profit margins over a number of years is a strong indication that the company is doing well.

A company that is profitable will be able to pay its liabilities as they fall due. Profitable companies are also capable of distributing and grow dividends to investors. However, be careful not to take everything at face value: it does not tell the whole story. You still have to look into the reasons for the increase or decrease to get a clearer, better, and more accurate picture of the business' profitability and overall financial performance.

## WHAT DOES GROSS PROFIT MARGIN MEAN?

Gross Profit Margin is a financial metric used to assess a company's financial health and business model by revealing the proportion of money left over from revenues after accounting for the Cost of Goods Sold (COGS). Because it indicates how much money is available for innovation, expansion and increasing sales, it is vital that small businesses intending to grow show a high gross profit margin.

Gross Profit Margin is calculated as:

$$Gross\ Profit\ Margin = (Revenue - COGS) / Revenue$$

Examples of COGS include:

- Labour directly tied to production
- Depreciation of the manufacturing plant
- Utilities of the facilities tied to production
- Direct materials needed for the production of goods and services

## WHAT DOES OPERATING PROFIT MARGIN MEAN?

The operating margin is earnings before interest and taxes (EBIT) as a percentage of revenue, also known as EBIT margin. It is an indicator of a company's operational profitability. Higher operating margin indicates either that the company controls its costs or that sales increase quicker than costs of the operation. Having a high operating margin also means the company tends to generate substantial Free Cash Flow.

Operating Profit Margin is calculated as:

*Operating Profit Margin = Operating Profit / Revenue*

## WHAT DOES NET PROFIT MARGIN MEAN?

This is the ratio of earnings left after all costs and expenses have been deducted from gross sales or gross receipts. Unlike the Gross Profit Margin and the Operating Profit Margin, the Net Profit Margin takes into account the taxes as well as finance costs. It is essentially a reflection on how efficient the business is in using its resources in its operations and answers the question: how much, out of every buck in sales, is a company actually earning?

Net Profit Margin is calculated as:

*Net Profit Margin = Net Profit / Revenue*

## PROFIT MARGINS CHECKLIST

1. Is Gross Profit Margin higher than 50%?
2. Is operating margin (EBIT) above the industry average?
3. Has the average operating margin (EBIT) been higher than 15% for the past three years?
4. Has operating margin (EBIT) increased for three years in a row?
5. Has Net Profit Margin been positive in the past 10 years?
6. *Does the company have high operating leverage?*

**1. Is Gross Profit Margin higher than 50%?**

*Why does it matter?*

This check indicates if the company has a profitable product mix that is in high demand. A high gross margin is a sign of a business that can make a reasonable profit on sales, as long as it keeps overhead costs in control. The higher it is, the more profits will accelerate with sales growth. Also, a high gross margin allows the business to fund the investments out of their own cash flow. For a start-up it simply means that it will generate positive cash flow and profits when it does get to scale.

Gross margins vary widely based on industry and different companies use different expenses but in general, the higher the better. Nonetheless, we want a company to have gross margins higher than 50%.

*How to assess it?*

If the normalised Gross Profit Margin (see note below) is higher than 50%, the stock is scored one point.

NOTE: Gross margins can be quite misleading. For instance, a company must often front lower margin implementation/training costs to get a customer up and running. Accordingly, a company that is doing gangbuster business may see a material decline in Gross Profit Margin.

## 2. Is operating margin (EBIT) above the industry average?

*Why does it matter?*

This check indicates financial efficiency as it measures how efficiently a company manages expenses. The operating margin is independent of how the company is financed or taxed and is thus most suitable for profitability comparisons.

In general, companies that can perform above their industry's average are doing something right. And when margins are slim and tough times surface, as they always do from time to time, weak margin companies will probably start burning cash rather than generating it.

*How to assess it?*

If the past year's operating margin is higher than the relevant industry average, the stock is scored one point.

## 3. Has the average operating margin (EBIT) been higher than 15% for the past three years?

*Why does it matter?*

This check is used to identify companies with decent profit margins by looking at the operating margin. Though the preferable range for operating margin depends on the industry, we prefer a high operating margin as it leaves room for the business to stay profitable during bad times, when a low profit-margin business may fall into loss – something that usually inflicts major punishment on its stock price.

*How to assess it?*

If the average operating margin for the past three years is higher than 15%, the stock is scored one point. If the operating margin is 15%, or below, or no operating profit has been reported for at least three years, it scores no points.

## 4. Has operating margin (EBIT) increased for three years in a row?

*Why does it matter?*

This check is used as marginal incremental profitability over time indicates that the company is scaling nicely, as profits are growing faster than revenue. On the contrary, eroding profit margins are a cause for concern. Companies that are increasing their profit margins while they grow can carry very high valuation multiples, as future periods will have much higher earnings and free cash flow due to the cumulative effect of growth and increased profitability.

*How to assess it?*

If the past year's operating margin is positive and has increased for at least three years in a row, the stock is scored one point. If the margin is not increasing or no annual operating profits have been reported for each of the last three years, it scores no points.

## 5. Has Net Profit Margin been positive over the past 10 years?

*Why does it matter?*

This check reflects the stability of earnings being more important than their absolute number. Companies that have generated profits in each of the past 10 years can be considered more predictable and robust, demonstrating the ability to navigate recessions and industry slowdowns. Consequently, old age is typically an asset as the longer a company has been around the longer it should last in the future.

All else equal, we prefer to hold businesses that sell products with more stable demand. However, profit margins that fluctuate over a period of time are a tell-tale indicator of a business that is prone to periodic price wars and/or is highly cyclical (where sales move up and down in line with the overall economy).

*How to assess it?*

If Net Profits have been reported for at least 10 consecutive years, the stock is scored one point.

### 6. *Does the company have high operating leverage?*

*Why does it matter?*

This check measures the company's operating risk as the sensitivity in operating profits (EBIT) to its sales. This is a good thing when sales are increasing, but the process also works in reverse and will decimate profits when sales fall. In economic downturns, high operating leverage readily translates into rapidly deteriorating cash flows and difficulty meeting debt obligations.

Essentially, a high operating leverage says that a company has fixed costs and needs to keep making incremental profits or else it would risk making losses. Whereas a negative operating leverage ratio suggests inefficiencies in operations, as expenses are accumulating faster than sales.

*How to assess it?*

If the last quarter (year-over-year basis) Degree of Operating Leverage (DOL) is greater than 2, this check is flagged.

Degree of Operating Leverage is calculated as:

*Degree of Operating Leverage = % Change in Operating Profit / % Change in Sales*

This factor has a zero-weight impact on the scoring model for Financials and is included as additional information to assist with investment decision-making.

## FINANCIAL INSTITUTIONS

This analysis is used for financial institutions as they are different from other types of companies and have specific ratios to analyse profit margins – such as Net Interest Margin (NIM) and Efficiency Ratio. Keep in mind that the main objective of financial institutions is to act as an intermediary between those who have funds and those who seek funds for running their business or for personal use.

The first two checks from the profit margin checks above (Check #1 and #2) are replaced with more specific ratios and criteria, designed to suit financial institutions' unique business operations.

## WHAT DOES NET INTEREST MARGIN (NIM) MEAN?

This banking metric is analogous to Gross Profit Margin for non-financial companies. Banking is unique in its use of this term because its gross profit margin considers how much the bank has to pay depositors and debt holders for deposits and debt (bank liabilities), and how much the bank earns from borrowers and investments (assets). Moreover, a bank's NIM reflects its strategy as well as the business environment.

Net Interest Margin is calculated as:

> *Net Interest Margin = Interests Earned on Loans and Investments - Total Interest Paid on Deposits and Debt*

## WHAT DOES EFFICIENCY RATIO MEAN?

This is a standard banking metric that shows investors how effectively banks are managing non-interest expenses. For example, it captures various aspects that translates into lower non-interest expenses, such as cheaper rental payments for premises and fewer bad-credit problems. This makes efficiency ratios important, because improvement in them usually translates to improved profitability.

Efficiency Ratio is calculated as:

*Efficiency Ratio = Non-interest Expenses / Revenue*

## PROFIT MARGINS CHECKLIST (FINANCIAL INSTITUTIONS)

1. Is Net Interest Margin (NIM) above the industry average?
2. Is the Efficiency Ratio below 60%?

FINANCIAL INSTITUTIONS

### 1. Is Net Interest Margin (NIM) above the industry average?

*Why does it matter?*

This check measures the difference between interest income generated and interest expenses. Unlike most other companies, the bulk of a bank's income and expenses is created by interest. Since the bank funds a majority of its operations through customer deposits, it pays out a large total amount in interest expense. The majority of its revenue is derived from collecting interest on loans.

*How to assess it?*

To decide whether a financial institution is performing better or worse than the industry average, compare institutions within the same country, as there are substantial differences in this ratio between countries.

If the current year Net Interest Margin is greater than the industry average, the stock is scored one point.

FINANCIAL INSTITUTIONS

## 2. Is the Efficiency Ratio below 60%?

*Why does it matter?*

This check indicates how good a financial institution is at using its assets to generate revenue, as it measures the amount of non-interest expense it takes to create a buck in revenue. The ratio does not include interest expenses, as these occur naturally when deposits grow. However, non-interest expenses, such as marketing or operational expenses, can be controlled by the bank. A decrease in the ratio equates to better expense performance, so the lower the ratio, the better. Being a low-cost producer is a tremendous competitive advantage in an industry like banking. Hence, there is a clear correlation between bank size and efficiency ratios.

*How to assess it?*

If the Efficiency Ratio is below 60%, the stock is scored one point.

# GROWTH RATES ANALYSIS

## DOES THE COMPANY HAVE A STRONG GROWTH TREND?

A company that grows its revenues and earnings consistently and rapidly will be worth more than a volatile and slow-growing company – but only if they have the same reinvestment capacity, are earning the same rate of return on invested capital and as long as this rate of return is materially higher than the opportunity cost of capital.

If a company's earnings bounce all over the place, it's either in an extremely volatile industry or it's regularly getting attacked by competitors. However, the growth rates usually shed light on how the company's operations are doing and how they are growing. For example, sales growth is a good representation of a company's ability to take market share and/or participate in a growing industry. And EPS growth is an indication of a company's ability to increase earnings – whether through better sales, good control of expenses or a combination thereof.

It should be noted that the growth rate analysis is very specifically designed to be 'predictive' rather than 'descriptive'. It is more focused on the near-term growth trend as research shows that the historical long-term growth rate is not very predictive of future stock returns. Growth tends to naturally slow down as a company gains size over time. Accordingly, a high growth stock is essentially a description of a development stage in a company's life cycle.

## WHAT DOES REVENUE GROWTH MEAN?

Also referred as sales, revenue is income that a company receives from its normal business activities, usually from the sale of goods and services to customers. Revenue is often referred to as the 'top line' due to its position at the very top of the income statement.

Revenue growth is used to measure how fast a company's business is expanding. The figure shows the annual rate of increase/decrease in a company's revenue or sales growth, typically based on either trailing 12 months or three years. All things being equal, stocks with higher revenue growth rates are generally more desirable than those with slower revenue growth rates. A high growth rate indicates low saturation and high demand, whereas a negative rate could suggest that consumers are losing interest in the product.

Genuine growth stocks grow revenues 10% or more annually with rising or high reinvestment rates of at least 20%. However, to justify paying up for growth investors need more than price leverage. It takes high unit growth as well.

## WHAT DOES EARNINGS GROWTH MEAN?

The Earnings Growth Rate is the percentage change in a company's Earnings per Share (EPS) in a period, as compared with the same period from the previous year. Earnings growth gives a good picture of a company's growth prospects. All things being equal, stocks with better growth prospects are more desirable than those with poorer growth rates.

## WHAT DOES RETENTION RATIO MEAN?

The Retention Ratio (also called the Plowback Ratio) is the proportion of earnings kept back in the business as retained earnings. It refers to the percentage of net income that is retained to grow the business, rather than being paid out as dividends. Without a steady reinvestment rate, company growth would be completely dependent on financing from investors and creditors.

In a sense the Retention Ratio is the opposite of the Payout Ratio. It shows how much money the company chooses to keep in its bank account, whereas the Payout Ratio measures the percentage of profit paid out to shareholders as dividends. The Retention Ratio increases retained earnings while the Payout Ratio decreases retained earnings.

Retention Ratio is calculated as:

*Retention Ratio = Net Profit - Dividends / Net Profit*

## GROWTH RATES CHECKLIST

1. Is the annual Retention Ratio above 70%?
2. Has annual growth rate in revenue been consistently above the industry average?
3. Is the annual growth rate in revenue above 15%?
4. Is annual growth in earnings (EPS) above 15%?
5. Have earnings (EPS) increased in each of the past five years?
6. *Have earnings (EPS) grown at an extreme rate over the last three years?*

**1. Is the annual Retention Ratio above 70%?**

*Why does it matter?*

This check indicates whether the company retain most of its profits to reinvest and grow the business. A growth-oriented company that aims to expand, develop new products, and move into new markets would be expected to retain most or all of its profits.

A high ratio doesn't necessarily mean the company is investing those funds back into its own business or other businesses at above-average rate of return. This is a more efficient way of compounding shareholders' capital than paying out dividends. A low rate typically coincides with a lack of reinvesting opportunities, and consequently a slower revenue and earnings growth.

*How to assess it?*

If the average Retention Ratio over the last three years is above 70%, the stock is scored one point. If no Net Profit has been reported in any of the last three years, it scores no points.

## 2. Has annual growth rate in revenue been consistently above the industry average?

*Why does it matter?*

Annual growth rates that are above the industry average growth rate indicates that the company is winning market share, and on the other hand below the average figure means declining market share. While long-term market share gain is a strong sign of a quality company, market share shifts are usually most pronounced during economic busts when times are tough. Look for the strongest players to come out of slowdowns with more share than the marginal players.

Revenue per share is an important metric because it's unaffected by most one-time items that can help or hurt earnings per share. It also takes into account the effect of dilution from stock issuance, as well as lower numbers of shares outstanding due to buybacks.

*How to assess it?*

If annual revenue growth (adjusted for M&A) is greater than the relevant industry average in each of the last five years, the stock is scored one point.

## 3. Is the annual growth rate in revenue above 15%?

*Why does it matter?*

This check is used to identify growth companies by looking at the annual growth rate of its revenues. Revenue growth is a purer measure of growth, as the number is more difficult to manipulate. While a high growth rate indicates low saturation and high demand, a negative rate could suggest that consumers are losing interest in the company's product.

*How to assess it?*

If compound annual growth in revenues over the last three years is greater than 15%, the stock is scored one point. If fewer than four years of revenues are available, it scores no points.

The compound annual growth rate (CAGR) formula is the following:

*Compound Annual Growth Rate (CAGR) of Revenues = (current year's Sales growth / Sales growth 3 years ago) ^ (1/3) – 1*

## 4. Is annual growth in earnings (EPS) above 15%?

*Why does it matter?*

This check is used to identify good growth companies by looking at the annual growth rate of earnings. Earnings growth indicates whether the company is able to grow its profitability, which impacts the valuation of the company fundamentally. Yet growth stocks have finite lives, typically five to 10 years. Very high growth rates are usually achieved by young companies and growth rates of mature companies are much more moderate.

*How to assess it?*

This growth rate is the compound annual growth rate of diluted normalised earnings per share over the last three years. In the 'normalised' EPS figure, one-off, non-recurring or exceptional items are subtracted from the reported EPS figure to give a more accurate depiction of the company's underlying profitability.

If compound annual growth in Earnings per Share over the last three years is greater than 15%, the stock is scored one point. If fewer than four years of positive earnings are available, it scores no points.

The compound annual growth rate (CAGR) formula is the following:

*CAGR of Earning per Share (EPS) = (current year's EPS growth / EPS growth 3 years ago) ^ (1/3) − 1*

## 5. Have earnings (EPS) increased in each of the past five years?

*Why does it matter?*

This check is used as stable growth in Earnings per Share (EPS) year after year typically means higher predictability. Companies in cyclical industries may see their EPS fluctuate wildly in good years and bad years. All else equal, we prefer to hold businesses that sell products with more stable demand. These companies often have more within their control and produce steadier earnings growth.

*How to assess it?*

If the company hasn't suffered an EPS loss or decline in any of the last five years, the stock is scored one point.

## 6. Have earnings (EPS) grown at an extreme rate over the last three years?

*Why does it matter?*

This check is used to identify if a company is experiencing extreme earnings growth. The destiny of any fast-growing business is to experience a growth rate that eventually slows down. In other words, earnings growth is generally mean-reverting over time.

Growth stocks' trajectory towards maturity normally lasts no more than five years, typically because they lose their dominance. Only a handful manage to reign for more than a decade (see note below).

Investors systematically overvalue high-growth companies as they generally expect too much of the future. As a result, the fastest-growing companies often fail to live up to expectations and can witness the biggest earnings disappointments. Accordingly, you should generally avoid the most aggressive growth companies as they are the most vulnerable to overvaluation, multiple fade, and competitive business pressures.

*How to assess it?*

If compound annual growth in Earnings per Share over the last three years is greater than 50%, the stock is flagged.

The compound annual growth rate (CAGR) formula is the following:

$$CAGR \text{ of Earnings per Share (EPS)} = (\text{current year's EPS growth} / \text{EPS growth 3 years ago})^{\wedge} (1/3) - 1$$

This factor has a zero-weight impact on the scoring model and is included as additional information to assist with investment decision-making.

NOTE: A company with rapidly growing sales and earnings can perform very well for a time despite seemingly higher valuations.

However, sustaining high annual sales growth is extremely difficult as the law of large numbers naturally causes many companies to end their growth streak. On average only one company in the S&P500 was able to sustain 10%+ sales growth for 10 consecutive years between 1990 and 2015.

# FINANCIAL HEALTH ANALYSIS

## IS THE COMPANY IN GOOD FINANCIAL CONDITION?

Many investment mistakes can be traced to overlooking the company's financial position – in particular, the downside risks of debt or its sources. Debt can be seductive because even investors wary of excessive leverage can be deceived into stressing its upside more than its downside. However, debt can be the biggest enemy of investors as lenders always get paid before shareholders.

Debt-oriented mistakes are most likely during periods of economic expansion. During prosperity, even mediocre companies appear to perform exceptionally well. Through such frothy periods, market valuations tend to be high and it can be tempting to compromise on issues such as leverage. But it's the companies with solid balance sheets that can weather economic downturns, make opportunistic acquisitions, waste less of their profit on debt interest, absorb unexpected problems with ease and keep moving forward.

## WHAT DOES DEBT TO EQUITY RATIO MEAN?

Debt to equity is also known as the Gearing Ratio. Debt in this case usually refers to short and long-term interest-bearing debt, such as bank loans. The lower the ratio is, the lower the risk of failure or bankruptcy. A low debt indicates that the company's operations are financed internally, through earnings from operations. Ideally, the company will hold no debt, but debt is generally a cheaper way to grow than through equity and allows growth beyond the capabilities of current cash inflows from operating activities.

Debt to equity is calculated as:

$$Debt\ to\ Equity = Net\ Debt\ /\ Total\ Book\ Value\ of\ Shareholders'\ Equity$$

## WHAT DOES INTEREST COVERAGE RATIO MEAN?

The Interest Coverage Ratio, also known as times interest earned, is used to determine how easily a company can pay interest on its outstanding debt relative to its operating profitability (EBIT). A higher ratio means that the organization has sufficient buffer even after paying interest. The earnings, tax and interest figures are found on the income statement.

Interest Coverage Ratio is calculated as:

$$Interest\ Coverage\ Ratio = EBIT\ /\ Net\ Interest\ Expense$$

## WHAT DOES CASH FLOW FROM OPERATIONS MEAN?

Cash Flow from Operations (CFO), often called Operating Cash Flow (OCF), tells you how much cash flow has been generated by the core operations of the business. It excludes cash flows from investing and financing in order to focus on the cash flows for the ongoing operations which will determine the long-term success of the company. In the long run CFO must be positive for the company to remain solvent.

Cash Flow from Operations is calculated as:

> *Cash Flow from Operations = Net Income + Depreciation + Adjustments to Net Income + Changes in Accounts Receivables + Changes in Liabilities + Changes in Inventories + Changes in other Operating Activities*

## WHAT DOES FREE CASH FLOW MEAN?

Free Cash Flow (FCF) measures how much cash is left over to a company's investors after all necessary investments to sustain its operations, such as investments in working capital and fixed capital, including plant, property and equipment, otherwise known as capital expenditures, plus any expenses required to remain a going concern. We are here focusing on capital spending that merely sustains its business, not CAPEX that expands the business. They are often lumped together, so you need to separate them. Accordingly, it involves judgement calls about the true level of maintenance spending.

FCF is an important measure because it allows a company to pursue opportunities that enhance shareholder value. Excess cash can expand production, develop new products, make acquisitions, pay dividends and reduce debt. Conversely, if FCF is negative, a business burns through cash reserves and eventually needs to raise funds via debt, new shares, or asset sales. In other words, companies can't survive over the long term without generating FCF.

Free Cash Flow is calculated as:

*Free Cash Flow = Cash Flow from Operations − Capital Expenditures*

## FINANCIAL HEALTH CHECKLIST

1. Are Current Assets 1.5 times greater than Current Liabilities?
2. Is Total Debt less than three times Operating Cash Flow?
3. Is Total Debt less than 10 times Free Cash Flow?
4. Is the Debt to Equity ratio below 50%?
5. Is interest on debt covered more than five times by earnings (EBIT)?
6. *Does the company underspend on maintaining its assets?*

### 1. Are Current Assets 1.5 times greater than Current Liabilities?

*Why does it matter?*

This check measures whether the company has the ability to service its short-term obligations or those due within one year from its current assets – cash, inventory, and any money coming into the company within 12 months.

*How to assess it?*

If the company's Current Assets are greater than 1.5x Current Liabilities, the stock is scored one point.

## 2. Is Total Debt less than three times Operating Cash Flow?

*Why does it matter?*

This check (Debt/OCF) indicates whether, in the event of financial stress, the company is able to meet its debt obligations using its cash flow from its operating activities. The Total Debt to OCF ratio simply shows how long it would take the company to pay back the debt if it stopped investing in its assets. This can only happen for a couple of years for most companies before their assets become worn out and need to be replaced. Therefore, with most companies you wouldn't really want to see a Total Debt to OCF ratio of more than 3.

*How to assess it?*

If Total Debt to Operating Cash Flow is less than 3.0, the stock is scored one point.

NOTE: Remember that debt levels on balance sheets are based on a snapshot on one particular day. Companies tend to present their year-end balance sheets when they give the most favourable picture of their financial position. Average debt levels can be a lot higher throughout the year.

One way of checking for this is to divide the cash interest paid figure in the cash flow statement with the total borrowings figure on the balance sheet. If the percentage figure is a big number – say more than 10% – then average debt levels are probably higher than year-end levels and the company has more debt than it is showing on its year-end balance sheet.

### 3. Is Total Debt less than 10 times Free Cash Flow?

*Why does it matter?*

This check (Debt/FCF) indicates how many years it would take to repay all the company's debt with the current rate of Free Cash Flow (FCF) it is producing. The lower the number, the better. Like all ratios, it is best looked at over a number of years to see if it is normal for the company to have a high value or if it is a recent trend.

*How to assess it?*

If Total Debt to Free Cash Flow is less than 10.0, the stock is scored one point.

## 4. Is the Debt to Equity ratio below 50%?

*Why does it matter?*

The Debt to Equity ratio measures the amount of ownership in a company (shareholders' equity) versus the amount of money owed to creditors (total liabilities). This ratio illustrates the level of leverage. If the ratio is high, this indicates that the company has a high level of debt compared to its net worth and, in the event of financial stress, may experience difficulty meeting debt or interest obligations. In contrast, a low ratio allows the company to continue meeting its financial obligations, even when the economy is in a downturn.

*How to assess it?*

If Debt to Equity ratio is less than 50%, the stock is scored one point.

NOTE: If the company belongs to a very cyclical industry, more equity is needed for an optimum balance sheet construct. Moreover, it's a bad sign if the ratio of debt to equity is rising and earnings are flat to down.

## 5. Is interest on debt covered more than five times by earnings (EBIT)?

*Why does it matter?*

This check indicates whether the company's interest obligations in the next five years are met through current year's earnings before interest and taxes (EBIT). A ratio of five times earnings indicates an acceptable level of interest coverage. It means that profits can fall by at least 40% before the ratio starts getting into the danger zone, which is considered as interest cover of three or less. Also, high levels of interest cover typically mean the company doesn't pay out too much in dividends, but rather re-invests earnings to compound growth over the long term.

*How to assess it?*

If EBIT (last twelve months) is more than 5 x interest on debt, the stock is scored one point.

### 6. Does the company underspend on maintaining its assets?

*Why does it matter?*

This check is used to identify if a company is spending enough to maintain its existing assets and keep them in good condition. In short it means that the company is spending less on capital expenditures (CAPEX) than its depreciation and amortisation expenses for several years, as a single year's CAPEX might not be representative of normal spending.

Typically, CAPEX items cover purchase of plants and production facilities, equipment, vehicles, etc, but may also include items such as money spent to purchase other companies or for research and development. Accordingly, you should consider amortisation as the equivalent of depreciation, but for intangible assets.

Sometimes you will come across a company where CAPEX spending is considerably below the depreciation and amortisation expenses on a regular basis and it will not be a problem due to the nature of the business.

*How to assess it?*

You can tell if the company underspend to maintain its existing assets, if the company is spending less on capital expenditures than its depreciation and amortisation. Ideally capital expenditures should exceed depreciation and amortisation expenses over time.

Some companies will differentiate between capital expenditures needed for growth and capital expenditures needed to maintain the business. Yet, they are often lumped together, so you need to separate them by making judgement calls about the true level of maintenance spending.

If the company is spending less on maintenance CAPEX than its depreciation and amortisation expenses for the last year and the maintenance CAPEX-to-Depreciation-and-Amortisation ratio (CAPEX to D&A) is below its average over the last five years, the stock is flagged.

This factor has a zero-weight impact on the scoring model for Financials and is included as additional information to assist with investment decision-making.

## CASH RUNWAY ANALYSIS

This analysis is used for companies that have been loss-making on average over the past three years. An important factor to consider when analysing a loss-making company is the sustainability of its operations at its current level of cash, given that its revenues do not cover its costs.

For loss-making companies, the last three of the balance sheet checks above (Check #4, #5 and #6) are replaced with more stringent and relevant criteria.

## FINANCIAL HEALTH CHECKLIST (LOSS-MAKING COMPANIES)

4. Do cash and short-term investments cover expected cash burn (negative Free Cash Flow) for more than two years?
5. Is the company likely to become sustainably cash flow-positive this or next year?
6. *Does the company need to raise cash in the capital markets within 12 months?*

LOSS-MAKING COMPANIES

### 4. Do cash and short-term investments cover expected cash burn (negative Free Cash Flow) for more than two years?

*Why does it matter?*

This check indicates whether the company's cash and other liquid asset levels are sufficient to cover its negative Free Cash Flow over the next two years. This typically means that the company is liquid enough to withstand a market crisis and that it doesn't need to raise cash for at least a year.

*How to assess it?*

If Net Profit has been negative in at least two of the last three reported years and if coverage is sufficient (cash and cash equivalents expected costs) for the next two years, the stock is scored one point.

LOSS-MAKING COMPANIES

## 5. Is the company likely to become sustainably cash flow-positive this or next year?

*Why does it matter?*

This check indicates whether the company is likely to achieve sustainably cash flow-positive operations this or next year. It means that the company is at an inflection point to be funded by its customers rather than investors. This is the ultimate validation of the business model, something that may attract new less speculative investors – particularly if it offers high positive operating leverage.

*How to assess it?*

If Net Profit has been negative in at least two of the last three years and positive free cash flow is forecast for the current or next year and the following two years, the stock is scored one point.

LOSS-MAKING COMPANIES

## 6. Does the company need to raise cash in the capital markets within 12 months?

*Why does it matter?*

This check indicates whether there is high likelihood that management will be forced to raise additional funds within 12 months or less, as they are running out of operating cash. With such a short time frame it will likely require a deep discount (i.e. potentially creating a bargain opportunity) to get investors to fund the operating deficit. Nonetheless, this suggests that you should stay away, at least until the issue is solved, as good companies should never find themselves running out of cash. The bottom line is that if the company has to raise capital to meet its financing and operational needs, oftentimes this capital is very expensive and dilutive to existing shareholders.

*How to assess it?*

If Net Profit has been negative in the last 12 months and Net Profit coverage is not sufficient for the next 12 months, the stock is flagged.

This factor has a zero-weight impact on the scoring model for Financials and is included as additional information to assist with investment decision-making.

## FINANCIAL INSTITUTIONS

This analysis is used in the case of banks, financial service companies, and insurance companies, because their business model is different from others. Loans are an asset for a financial institution since they earn interest income from lending. Hence, a financial institution is only as good as the quality of its loans. The riskier the loan portfolio, the greater the risk of loan defaults which jeopardizes long-term profits for a financial institution.

Considering that banking is a semi-commodity business, the industry suffers from skinny margins. Consequently, fewer lending mistakes is critical as it means that less operating costs are tied up in collections, work-out personnel, lawyer fees, and loan officers whose attention is diverted from getting new businesses to overseeing the bad credit.

The bottom line is that the chief risk with investing in a financial institution is bad loans, as not every loan an institution lends out will get repaid. Moreover, considering the leverage involved, a questionable leadership character of a financial institution poses a much higher risk than most other, relatively unleveraged, businesses.

Since financial health is especially important for financial institutions, there are several ratios to measure its ability to pay off its debts over the long term. Consequently, you should use a checklist unique to financial institutions to assess if one is in good financial condition – see the following pages.

# FINANCIAL HEALTH CHECKLIST (FINANCIAL INSTITUTIONS)

1. Is Leverage (Assets to Equity) less than 15 times?
2. Is the Common Equity Tier 1 (CET1) ratio above 10%?
3. Does the institution have a strong Texas ratio?
4. Is Non-Performing Loan exposure less than 2%?
5. Have Net Charge-Offs been consistently lower than peers'?
6. *Has deposit growth stagnated or declined over the past three years?*

FINANCIAL INSTITUTIONS

**1. Is Leverage (Assets to Equity) less than 15 times?**

*Why does it matter?*

This check evaluates if the company has acceptable levels of leverage. Leverage refers to the amount of assets held in a business when compared to the company's own resources (shareholders' equity). When assets are 15 times equity or higher, the leverage is considered excessive. That means if just 6.7% (1/15) of a bank's loans aren't repaid, those losses will destroy 100% of the bank's equity. Remember that an institution's equity capital is a cushion against downturns in the business cycle, i.e. against bad loans that result in charge-offs.

*How to assess it?*

If total assets are less than 15x shareholders' equity, the stock is scored one point.

FINANCIAL INSTITUTIONS

## 2. Is the Common Equity Tier 1 (CET1) ratio above 10%?

*Why does it matter?*

This check gauges the institution's financial strength, its ability to absorb unexpected losses or remain liquid in the event of a crisis. It is a measure of Common Equity Tier 1 capital (high-quality equity) as a percentage of risk-weighted assets. CET1 capital is considered the most loss-absorbing form of a financial institution's capital as it can be readily converted into cash to cover any exposures in the event of a wind-up.

*How to assess it?*

If the CET1 ratio is higher than 10%, it is considered low risk, the stock is scored one point. You can find this information in the financial institution's last quarterly report.

The formula for the CET1 ratio is:

*Common Equity Tier 1 ratio = (Tier 1 Capital - Preferred Stock - Noncontrolling Interests) / (Total Risk Adjusted Assets)*

NOTE: The required level of 4.5% is mandated under Basel III, which is an internationally agreed upon set of measures created by the Basel Committee on Banking Supervision to ensure stability in the global banking sector. This requirement was developed in response to the financial crisis of 2007-08.

FINANCIAL INSTITUTIONS

## 3. Does the institution have a strong Texas ratio?

*Why does it matter?*

This check gauges the riskiness of a financial institution's loan portfolio by the so-called Texas ratio. When the economy is strong, this ratio is typically low. When the economy falls into recession, Texas ratios typically rise. A ratio of more than 100% is sign that the risk of failure is very high and between 50% and 100% the institution is considered vulnerable.

NOTE: The reason it is known as the 'Texas ratio' is because it became prominent during the 1980s when more than 800 Texas banks failed. The bank analyst who came up with this ratio first applied it to Texas banks. Generally speaking, Texas banks overextended credit and lowered lending standards to booming energy and real estate sectors.

*How to assess it?*

If the Texas ratio is below 50%, or below 100% and has been decreasing over the last year, the stock is scored one point. You can find this information in the financial institution's last quarterly report.

Texas ratio is calculated as:

*Texas ratio = (Non-Performing Loans + Real Estate Owned) / (Tangible Common Equity + Loan Loss Reserves)*

WHERE:

*Non-Performing Loan*s = loans that are close to default, as they are more than 90 days past due and are not backed by the government.

*Tangible Common Equity* = a company's physical capital, which is used to evaluate a financial institution's ability to deal with potential losses. Tangible Common Equity is calculated by subtracting intangible assets and preferred equity from the company's book value.

FINANCIAL INSTITUTIONS

## 4. Is Non-Performing Loan exposure less than 2%?

*Why does it matter?*

This check indicates high overall quality of the institution's loan stock, that the institution has sound underwriting practices. In contrast, high non-performing loans (NPLs) indicates that the institution's credit department is rather lax in granting loans, not checking the credibility of the borrower properly. An institution with high NPLs tends to do well when the economy is doing well. However, it suffers when the economy goes south as borrowers who could afford the loans in better times suddenly start defaulting on their payments.

*How to assess it?*

If the NPL ratio is less than 2%, the stock is scored one point. You can find this information in the financial institution's last quarterly report.

Non-Performing Loan (NPL) ratio is calculated as:

*Non-Performing Loan (NPL) ratio = Total Non-Performing Loans / Total Outstanding Loans*

WHERE:

Non-Performing Loans = loans that are close to default, as they are more than 90 days past due and are not backed by the government.

FINANCIAL INSTITUTIONS

## 5. Have Net Charge-Offs been consistently lower than peers'?

*Why does it matter?*

This check indicates prudent underwriting practices, as it measures the performance of its loan portfolio in relation to its peers over time. The Net Charge-Off (NCO) ratio shows the amount of debt that an institution believes that it will never get back when compared to the average receivables. This typically happens when a borrower goes six months without making a payment.

Obviously, the lower the NCO rate, the better. But it's important to view this number in the context of the current credit cycle – credit losses tend to increase during periods of economic stress, so you want to view NCO rates across institutions to see where a financial institution falls in relation to its peers over time.

*How to assess it?*

If the Net Charge-Off ratio is lower than the relevant industry average for every single year of the last five, the stock is scored one point. You can find this information in the financial institution's annual and quarterly reports.

Net Charge-Off (NCO) ratio is calculated as:

$$Net\ Charge\text{-}Off\ (NCO)\ ratio = Net\ Charge\text{-}Offs\ /\ Total\ Loans$$

FINANCIAL INSTITUTIONS

## 6. Has deposit growth stagnated or declined over the past three years?

*Why does it matter?*

This check indicates potential funding difficulties as the institution will have less money to lend if deposit growth has stagnated, or if its deposits are shrinking. After all, deposits are the raw material that an institution uses to make its finished goods – interest income.

To meet the credit needs of their customers, the bank has to supplement traditional funding sources with potentially less stable and more expensive funding instruments. In addition, the banks may take other significant steps, including cutting back on their holdings of cash and selling parts of their loan portfolio. All steps that will increase the challenges in maintaining a sound and profitable operation.

*How to assess it?*

If the deposits last year are less than 1x deposits from three years ago, this check is flagged. You can find this information in the financial institution's annual and quarterly reports.

This factor has a zero-weight impact on the scoring model for Financials and is included as additional information to assist with investment decision-making.

# EARNINGS QUALITY ANALYSIS
IS THE QUALITY OF THE COMPANY'S EARNINGS HIGH?

Earnings quality is about avoiding companies with aggressive accounting standards, as it is a symptom of poor management. The quality of earnings refers to the amount of earnings attributable to higher sales or lower costs, rather than artificial profits created by accounting anomalies or tricks such as inflation of inventories or changing depreciation or inventory methodology. In other words, you would do well to examine the accounting carefully and heed early warning signs.

The principal concern is whether the earnings have been overstated in financial statements. Earnings growth due to accrual growth is not sustainable and that's why careful assessment of earnings quality is critical, and not simply taking financial statements at their face value. Accruals are revenues and expenses that are incurred during an accounting period for which no invoices or payments were received or made. As the saying goes, 'revenue is vanity, profit sanity, cash is reality,' the chief lesson is that cash is king.

As an investor you should live by the notion that management is 'guilty until proven innocent' if there are any inconsistencies between the balance sheet, income statement, and cash flow statements. Particularly when there is a downturn in the economy and managers feel the pressure to meet earning expectations or debt covenants or to maintain or increase their personal wealth.

## WHAT DOES INVENTORY TO SALES MEAN?

Inventory to Sales is an efficiency ratio that is used to determine the rate at which the company is liquidating its inventory. It measures the amount of inventory a company is carrying compared to the number of sales orders being fulfilled. A high ratio indicates a high level of inventory and, consequently, a less efficient inventory performance. If the ratio rises, it indicates either that sales are falling or that the company is keeping too much inventory in stock, all of which are generally a negative sign. At the same time, if the inventory starts to build up, the costs to store and manage it will eat into the company's profits.

Inventory to Sales ratio is calculated as:

*Inventory to Sales ratio = Average Inventory / Net Sales*

**Where:**

*Average Inventory* = (Beginning Inventory + Ending Inventory) / 2

NOTE: We use the annual average inventory as it takes out any seasonality effects while calculating the ratio.

## WHAT DOES ACCOUNTS RECEIVABLES TO SALES MEAN?

The Accounts Receivables (AR) to Sales is a business liquidity ratio that measures how much of a company's sales occur on credit (unpaid sales). When a company has a larger percentage of its sales happening on a credit basis, it may run into short-term liquidity problems during difficult economic times and slow sales cycles. A high AR to sales ratio means a significant amount of cash is tied up with the slow paying customers. A low AR to sales ratio means that the business is generating fairly large cash flows from its operations, and thus relies less on its investing and financing activities for liquidity.

Accounts Receivables to Sales ratio is calculated as:

$$Accounts\ Receivables\ to\ Sales = Accounts\ Receivable\ /\ Sales$$

**Where:**

*Accounts Receivable* = sales that have occurred on credit, meaning that the company has not yet collected the cash proceeds from these sales. Found in the 'current assets' section of the balance sheet.

*Sales* = all sales that the company has realized over the given accounting period, including sales on credit and cash sales. Found on the income statement.

## EARNINGS QUALITY CHECKLIST

1. Does the company manage its inventory well?
2. Does the company manage its credit sales well?
3. Are one-time adjustments to earnings rare?
4. Does Cash Flow from Operations exceed Net Profit regularly?
5. Has the company consistently generated Free Cash Flow over the past five years?
6. *Was last year's income tax rate significantly lower than the statutory rate?*

∼

### 1. Does the company manage its inventory well?

*Why does it matter?*

This check is used to identify the trend in inventories, which companies need to control tightly. When there is a sudden and significant increase Inventory to Sales ratio, the company might be inflating the value of inventory. However, it could also mean that the company has failed to charge the cost of sales on some sales or is overproducing or is selling off its stocks as inventory may be obsolete and no longer in demand – any of which would be negative. It often indicates too that the company is facing larger financial problems.

*How to assess it?*

If the last four quarters' Inventory to Sales ratio is less than 1.1x the ratio in previous four quarters, the stock is scored one point. You can find this information in the balance sheet and income statement by the company's last eight quarterly reports.

## 2. Does the company manage its credit sales well?

*Why does it matter?*

This check indicates whether a company collects its credit sales competently. If accounts receivable gets significantly out of line with sales, it indicates clearly that the company is struggling to collect payments from customers and that the company might be inflating the value of receivables. Potential issues may be recording revenue too soon, or increased competition, forcing the company to extend better credit terms to customers. It's key to determine whether this is just a short term or cyclical abnormality or if there is a fundamental problem.

*How to assess it?*

If the last four quarters' Accounts Receivable to Sales ratio is less than 1.1x the ratio in previous four quarters, the stock is scored one point. You can find this information in the balance sheet and income statement by the company's last eight quarterly reports.

## 3. Are one-time adjustments to earnings rare?

*Why does it matter?*

This check indicates whether the company uses one-time adjustments to net profits infrequently. A multi-year pattern of significant one-time adjustments is a cause for concern that a company may be distorting its earnings performance to meet forecasts and that investors should question whether the underlying numbers have any value. After all, a one-time item, as the term implies, is supposed to be just that – a rare, infrequent event.

*How to assess it?*

If the one-time charges percentage of sales averaged less than 3% over the past five years, the stock is scored one point.

NOTE: Every time a company reports a one-time item, you should make sure that it is truly a one-off and that it is material enough that excluding it makes sense. As long as the item is indeed only a one-off, it may not lead to the company gaining the reputation of being a serial adjustor.

## 4. Does Cash Flow from Operations exceed Net Profit regularly?

*Why does it matter?*

This check is used to verify that the company is making not just accounting profits but cash profits. If Cash Flow from Operations (CFO) is consistently less than Net Profit, it might be a signal of heavy use of accrual accounting. In general, CFO should be higher than reported Net Profits as depreciation and amortisation are added back to Net Profit in the cash flow statement.

But if a company is growing very quickly or investing substantially in working capital, cash earnings are often less than accounting earnings. The bottom line: when companies report profits but bleed cash, believe the cash. Ultimately, if cash is not being generated the earnings are artificial.

*How to assess it?*

If Cash Flow from Operations to Net Profit is greater than 1 for at least three of the past five years, the stock is scored one point.

## 5. Has the company consistently generated Free Cash Flow over the past five years?

*Why does it matter?*

This check indicates whether the company's Free Cash Flow (FCF) is positive or negative. The latter means the company consumes more cash than it is taking in, which would require it to raise money by borrowing or offering additional new shares.

All the same time, negative FCF could also be a sign that a company is making significant investments. If these investments earn high returns, the strategy has the potential to add value in the long run.

*How to assess it?*

If FCF is positive in each of the past five years, the stock is scored one point.

## 6. Was last year's income tax rate significantly lower than the statutory rate?

*Why does it matter?*

This check indicates whether the earnings reported last year were potentially inflated by a lower level of income tax than the statutory corporate rate. This could be due to temporary deductibles like loss carry-forwards and/or tax benefits of interest deduction.

Note that this can be entirely legitimate for some companies because of conditions particular to them and/or their industry, such as subsidies, tax incentives and tax breaks.

*How to assess it?*

If the company's last year's annual income tax rate was less than 0.80x the statutory corporate tax rate, this check is flagged.

This factor has a zero-weight impact on the scoring model for Financials and is included as additional information to assist with investment decision-making.

# BRINGING IT ALL TOGETHER

# TIME FAVOURS QUALITY INVESTING

In a world where short-termism is encouraged by the power of algorithms and fuelled by thrill of rapid change, short-term performance can become an obsession and the longer outlook neglected. Identifying companies able to shrug off short-termism and gravity of financial theory means investing in quality stocks which are more likely to stand the test of time over the long term.

<u>Quality stocks tend to offer fewer negative surprises and, as a result, experience smaller falls than the overall market.</u> Accordingly, investing in quality companies helps avoid the unnecessary frustrations associated with recovering from steep losses. <u>But the real potential reward for investing in them is that high-quality companies continue growing over time by consistently reinvesting a large part of their earnings at high rates of return.</u> This compounds the value of your stake in the business over many years, achieving exponential growth. That's why great businesses are often referred to as compounders.

A business' compounding power can be analysed across three key dimensions:

- The percentage of earnings that can be reinvested back into the business
- The return on reinvested capital that the business can achieve
- How excess cash flow not reinvested in the business is used

For example, if a business can achieve 20% incremental returns on capital and reinvest 50% of its earnings each year, its intrinsic value will compound by 10% annually (20% x 50%). If it can buy back its shares at cheap levels or make value-accretive acquisitions with the other 50%, the compounding will be even stronger.

The bottom line is that with time on your side you don't have to go for home runs to invest successfully. You will do better paying fair value for a high-quality company and sticking with it. Timing is far less important. The 'rolling snowball' effect of compounding explains why the risks of permanently losing capital are low even if, in hindsight, you end up overpaying for great businesses. For a deeper explanation see 'Bringing Valuation into the Equation'.

Another great and more obvious advantage in buying high-quality stocks is low portfolio turnover. You allow the money you would have had to pay in capital gains taxes to continue compounding on your behalf. You also reduce transaction costs such as trading commission and slippage, while accruing dividends that you might otherwise miss by moving in and out of the market too quickly.

Only buying stocks for less than they are worth means that you are just speculating on an increase in its stock price, which have little to do with the underlying fundamentals. Stocks owned primarily because of price tend to be investments in poor quality companies. These requires constant focus on timing as they have to be sold fairly quickly. This is because any gap between price and value when you bought the stock slowly erodes over time as fair value declines due to the poor quality of the business.

This leads to a second problem with making investments primarily on the basis that the stock is cheap. Once it is fairly priced and sold you need to find a new opportunity, including doing all the necessary due diligence.

As a result, you can't keep using all of your previous research on an investment, even though the most valuable information usually has a long timeframe for which it is relevant (quality of the business model, potential growth opportunities, industry structure, management team track record etc.). Having to constantly generate new ideas by finding and analysing a lot of new information each time is a significant downside. On top of that, an investment approach that requires a lot of decision-making is more error-prone.

## BRINGING VALUATION INTO THE EQUATION

Having confidence in the long-term earnings trajectory of a business is one of the strongest edges you can have as an investor. <u>If you are right about the sustainability of a high-quality company's growth and profitability, you are probably buying the business at a very low multiple of future earnings.</u> This because you get both compounding from earnings growth and the reward of multiple expansion that typically follows a history of consistent earnings growth.

Earnings expectations for a business don't tend to vary significantly one year out, but opinions about the multiple that it deserves do. These are often focused on a belief that reversion to the mean is imminent without considering the business and company differences. It follows that forecasting current year earnings is key for investors with a short-term focus.

However, when looking further out, a company's valuation multiple is increasingly dependent on its longer-term earnings power and predictability. As a result, differences in earnings expectations and valuation multiples become more pronounced as market participants' varying assumptions compound over the long term.

Because of this, current valuation multiples should not be a major concern, if deep fundamental research supports sustainability of growth. If you are a long-term investor, your margin of safety has more to do with your confidence that a company's competitive advantages will stay strong or get stronger, rather than some estimate of a discount to its fair value. The important lesson to learn is that it's better to make a mistake on the purchase price of a business, than the quality of a business, as quality drives stock prices in the long run.

Using *the illustrative table below* as an example, if you pay 20x earnings for a 20% compounder in year 0, the corresponding margin of safety on your assumed exit multiple in year 10 is materially higher given the 3.2x effective forward P/E multiple on your investment. Consequently, you should pay up for high-quality companies that are able to maintain earnings growth year-after-year.

When you are a long-term investor in great businesses, what seems expensive on near-term multiples is often cheap in the long run. The fact is that despite having almost never appeared fairly valued, Amazon and Netflix are two of the best performing stocks of the past decade. As the investor Christopher Mayer once pointed out: "Don't let a seemingly high multiple scare you away from a great stock."

|  | YEAR | | | | | | |
|---|---|---|---|---|---|---|---|
| **EST EPS GROWTH** | 0 | 1 | 2 | 3 | 4 | 5 | 10 |
|  | EPS (€) | | | | | | |
| 0% | 1.00 | 1.00 | 1.00 | 1.00 | 1.00 | 1.00 | 1.00 |
| 5% | 1.00 | 1.05 | 1.10 | 1.16 | 1.22 | 1.28 | 1.63 |
| 10% | 1.00 | 1.10 | 1.21 | 1.33 | 1.46 | 1.61 | 2.59 |
| 15% | 1.00 | 1.15 | 1.32 | 1.52 | 1.75 | 2.01 | 4.05 |
| 20% | 1.00 | 1.20 | 1.44 | 1.73 | 2.07 | 2.49 | 6.19 |
|  | FORWARD P/E (ASSUMING BUYING AT 20X TO START) | | | | | | |
| 0% | 20.0X | 20.0X | 20.0X | 20.0X | 20.0X | 20.0X | 20.0X |
| 5% | 20.0X | 19.0X | 18.1X | 17.3X | 16.5X | 15.7X | 12.3X |
| 10% | 20.0X | 18.2X | 16.5X | 15.0X | 13.7X | 12.4X | 7.7X |
| 15% | 20.0X | 17.4X | 15.1X | 13.2X | 11.4X | 9.9X | 4.9X |

Source: Redeye Equity Research

A rational long-term investor with perfect foresight would pay up to a price where the future total return matches the return of the underlying market. Say the market compounds at 12%. This warrants a P/E multiple of 40 times earnings in year 0 (20 x 6.19 $1.12^{10}$), without considering multiple expansion. At that price, the future total return of the company would be equal to the market return over the subsequent 10 years.

In other words, when you overpay for quality, the period until the stock generates excess returns is prolonged as it will take a few years for the business to catch up with the stock. Peter Lynch once explained this, "Time is on your side when you own shares of superior companies."

# PATIENCE PAYS OFF IN INVESTING

Patience is a necessity when investing in great companies and the secret to making your money grow. All too often impatience costs investors dearly because they can't fight their emotions. Many end up buying at the tail end of a market rally or selling in a panic at a loss. However, <u>you must have patience to ride through the inevitable downswings, to wait for great investments to play out and let the power of compounding do its work.</u>

Likewise, <u>you have to have patience to wait for the right opportunity to buy at a price well below its fair value estimate.</u> Great companies are rarely available at cheap valuations. But once in a while you will be able to buy them at reasonable prices – especially during an economic downturn or a temporary setback.

In 1973 Warren Buffet invested more than US$10 million in The Washington Post Company. By the end of 1974 the share price had dropped nearly 25% and it took three years to recover fully. Instead of selling his stake while the price was falling, Buffet went against the herd and continued buying. He knew that the fundamentals of the business were strong and that the stock was cheap. Over time the share price bounced back and the business grew – and so did the underlying business value. Because of stock repurchases per-share business value increased considerably faster. Today Buffett regards his investment in the Washington Post as one of his best and most profitable ever.

Maintaining a multi-year view by focusing your thoughts on the long-term fundamentals and not expecting instant returns is probably the most important aspect of avoiding short-term noise. If Buffett had sold his Washington Post shares when the price fell, he would have lost money and missed out on the potential for future returns. That's why he is fond of saying that the stock market is a device for transferring money from the impatient to the patient. The important lesson is that if you have done your homework well in investing in a high-quality business, 'be patient and wait' remains the best stance in your pursuit of wealth creation from stocks.

The bottom line is that patience is the most essential investor quality, but also one of the hardest things to learn. As the legendary trader Jesse Livermore once said, "That is why so many men in Wall Street who are not at all in the 'sucker' class, not even in the third grade, nevertheless lose money. The market does not beat them. They beat themselves, because though they have brains, they cannot sit still."

## THE RATIONALITY OF HOLDING CASH

Remember: it's typically better to stay on the sidelines and wait for better opportunities than to commit to owning stocks priced for sub-par returns. It's critical to resist the pull of action that satisfies the itch to 'do something'. After all, to most of us, activity equals achievement. Likewise, in a bull market, we all hate the feeling of missing out on the party and avoid cash in favour of stocks. But then, as Charlie Munger says, "It takes character to sit there with all that cash and do nothing. I didn't get to where I am by going after mediocre opportunities."

Munger would go years building up huge cash reserves until he felt he had found something low-risk and highly intelligent. The bottom line is that keeping cash on hand facilitates an investor's success, even if it feels wrong to be sitting on it and earning nothing for long periods.

Holding cash is a cheap hedge as its value rise as the market plunges. And in addition to downside protection, cash also provides 'peace of mind' over large, unexpected costs or redemption requests by fund investors. It will certainly reduce the risk of panic-driven selling when markets get volatile. But most importantly, <u>always having cash available to invest enables you to take advantage of opportunities that may present themselves in the future without first needing to sell other stocks</u> – which would have likely become cheap themselves in a sell-off. The downside, of course, is losing purchasing power over time due to inflation and the risk of being underinvested in a rapidly rising market.

A common-sense strategy may be to allocate at least 5% of your portfolio to cash in a prevailing bull market, though many prudent money managers may prefer to keep between 10% and 20% in cash on average. It's all about how much volatility you can stomach. Everyone's temperament is different, so if investments are keeping you awake at night, <u>it is important to reduce the percentage invested down to your sleep level</u> – particularly when investing opportunities are scarce.

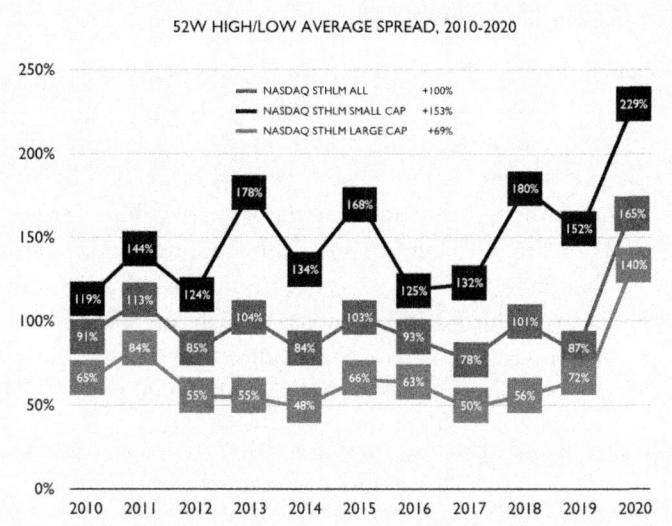

Source: Redeye Equity Research and Bloomberg

The average stock price fluctuates by roughly 100% annually, comparing 52-week low to 52-week high. This is based on the results from a volatility analysis on all stocks traded on Nasdaq Stockholm Exchange for the 2010-20 period, with 2020 being an outlier year due to the COVID-19 pandemic (see chart above). Clearly, the average business's underlying value doesn't fluctuate this much over a year. Moreover, the stock market loses 10% of its overall value about once per year on average. So, the patient investor usually doesn't have to wait more than a year or two for an attractive entry point, due to the volatility of the marketplace. In the meantime, building a watchlist of great companies to own at the right price is time well spent.

This quote from Warren Buffett is well worth remembering and serves as a fitting conclusion to this section: "Cash is like oxygen. When you don't need it, you don't notice it. When you do need it, it's the only thing you need."

## THE BEAUTY OF COMPOUNDING

Albert Einstein famously referred to compound interest – that is, the return on incremental capital – as the eighth wonder of the world. He also called it "mankind's greatest invention because it allows for the reliable, systematic accumulation of wealth." Although its power is relatively invisible over short periods of time, it is enormous over the long term. Keep in mind that more than 97% of Warren Buffett's net worth came after his 65th birthday. As noted, much of the secret to successful investing is the compounding of returns over time, as the table 'Compound Interest' below illustrates.

**COMPOUND INTEREST**

| | 20% SIMPLE GROWTH | | 20% COMPOUND GROWTH | |
|---|---|---|---|---|
| YEAR | PRINCIPAL | INTEREST | PRINCIPAL | INTEREST |
| 1 | 10,000 | 2,000 | 10,000 | 2,000 |
| 2 | 10,000 | 2,000 | 12,000 | 2,400 |
| 3 | 10,000 | 2,000 | 14,400 | 2,880 |
| 4 | 10,000 | 2,000 | 17,280 | 3,456 |
| 5 | 10,000 | 2,000 | 20,736 | 4,147 |
| 6 | 10,000 | 2,000 | 24,883 | 4,977 |
| 7 | 10,000 | 2,000 | 29,860 | 5,972 |
| 8 | 10,000 | 2,000 | 35,832 | 7,116 |
| 9 | 10,000 | 2,000 | 42,998 | 8,600 |
| 10 | 10,000 | 2,000 | 51,598 | 10,320 |
| TOTAL INTEREST | | 20,000 | | 51,917 |

Source: Redeye Equity Research

# PATIENCE PAYS OFF IN INVESTING

Harnessing the power of compounding will greatly impact your investment returns over time. Yet, people tend to confuse linear returns with the much more powerful exponential effect of compounding, which explains why the latter is often underestimated. After all, understanding that <u>a great company's stock can multiply 100 times in 25 years when you compound at 20% annually</u> is simple, but not intuitive. However, if you sell in year 20, you will get 'only' about 40 times. And if you hold it for just 10 years, your return is five times your original investment. But patiently sitting through these years earning an annual return of 20% is anything but easy. Along the way there are bumps in the road, plenty of naysayers and inevitable downswings. It takes a lot of conviction not to sell during those stressful times.

Thomas Phelps, provided a table in his truly fascinating book *100 to 1 in the Stock Market* that shows annual returns and how many years it would take before you achieve a 100-bagger:

**TIME NEEDED TO RETURN 100X**

| ANNUALISED RETURN (CAGR) | YEARS TO 100-BAGGER |
| --- | --- |
| 14% | 35 YEARS |
| 16.6% | 30 YEARS |
| 20% | 25 YEARS |
| 26% | 20 YEARS |
| 36% | 15 YEARS |

Source: 100 to 1 in the Stock Market, Thomas Phelps, 1972

A useful tool for assessing the impact of compound interest and the doubling effect is the Rule of 72. The rule says that if you divide an interest rate into 72, it will tell you how many years it will take to double your investment. At 24% interest, a buck would double in 3 years (72/24 = 3).

## THE UGLY SIDE OF COMPOUNDING

Just as compounding geometrically increases the value of positive returns, it also exacerbates the impact of negative returns. The bottom line is that it's very difficult to recover from a large loss or make up for negative-compounding years, to get you back to even. As rewards and penalties for compounding are asymmetrical, <u>what you should be aiming to accomplish is avoiding big mistakes</u>.

Winning big in the stock market is all about losing the least amount possible when you're wrong, not being right all the time. Remember, a seasoned investor who earns 20% for two consecutive years comes out ahead of a newbie investor who earns 100% in a bull year and loses 30% or more in the following year.

There is an old saying; "There are old pilots and there are bold pilots, but there aren't many old, bold pilots." The point is that you should always try to put yourself in a position where the likelihood of a big drop is extremely limited. As explained before, staying power counts in the investment world.

The ability to stick around for a long time should be the cornerstone of any investment strategy. That's why <u>you should avoid leverage (borrowed money) by using a cash-only account at your brokerage firm</u>. Leverage just magnifies outcomes, not adding value. Never forget that any stock you buy, or your whole portfolio, can go down 50% or more on the whims of the market. Leverage could literally destroy in a moment the benefit of many years of investment success by margin calls and forced sales from your brokerage firm.

Also, you should seek to <u>avoid overly leveraged investments and 'lottery tickets' – the get-rich-quick stocks – or at least ensure that these make up no more than a small portion of your portfolio</u>. In other words, keep your mistakes small enough so you can survive them; the upside takes care of itself.

The following table illustrates the asymmetrical impact of compounding – the more you lose, the harder it is to get back to even.

**LOSS/RECOVERY**

| PERCENT LOSS OF POSITION | RETURN NEEDED TO BREAK EVEN |
|---|---|
| -10% | 11% |
| -20% | 25% |
| -30% | 43% |
| -40% | 67% |
| -50% | 100% |
| -60% | 150% |
| -70% | 233% |
| -80% | 400% |
| -90% | 900% |

Source: Redeye Equity Research

However, interrupting the compounding clock can occur in many ways. Another common mistake is abandoning an investment strategy that has worked reasonably well over the long term, but recently had a few bad years. Moving on when things get tough to the hot new thing is likely to leave you worse off. Still, this investment failure is common as most investors have a year-end focus. It is intuitive to feel that the pursuit of the best returns at all times is the best way to maximise wealth. Nonetheless, maximising annual returns in a given year and maximising long-term wealth are two different things.

If the average investor is trying to win in the next year, and you trying to win over the next five years, you both have potential to win. But you are ultimately going to outperform by resisting the urge to 'swing for the fences'. <u>Successful investing is not about beating the market every time: it's about beating the market over time</u>. Short holding periods and the desire for quick gains are rather hallmarks of speculation. In other words, stock market investing is a long-term game that is best played over your entire lifetime.

## THE MISTAKE OF SELLING TOO EARLY

As Charlie Munger says, "the first rule of compounding is to never interrupt it unnecessarily." <u>The mistakes that will impact your performance most when investing in compounders are likely to be decisions to sell too soon</u>. One of the most powerful concepts in portfolio management is to let your winners run. Being a long-term investor can be relatively easy during a bull market. However, when the stock market gets extremely volatile, your resilience will be tested. After all, investing is an existential act. You are what you do, not what you think.

The bottom line is that <u>you can borrow ideas, but you can't borrow confidence or conviction</u>. You will never hold the compounders long enough to achieve stellar returns if you don't understand what you own, why you own it, and its value. You need deep industry expertise (past work) or recent analysis (current work) and the correct mindset to withstand the pain of extreme paper losses. Crisis conditions and headlines in the financial press often erode investors' patience, leading them to sell out of fear and lack of knowledge. Keep in mind that this is the key reason for doing deep fundamental research, to forge the courage to hold on to or buy into stocks after they have detached from reality on the downside.

Building real depth of knowledge about the company behind the stock is what makes part-time investing so difficult and why most retail investors struggle with stock selection. However, this is also the case for many professional money managers who have too many stocks in their portfolios. Very few have time to do deep dives on more than 20 companies, let alone maintain a superior understanding of all those portfolio holdings. Nonetheless, above-average investing is nearly impossible if you don't do the deep fundamental work to invest with high confidence and conviction.

Having more than 20 positions in your portfolio typically makes you more of a tourist than an owner in most of your positions. An owner's mindset is key to reap the benefits of compounding. Keep in mind the quote from the oil baron Paul Getty, "To succeed in business, to reach the top, an individual must know all it is possible to know about that business."

Selling compounders prematurely can be a life-altering mistake. Typically, a few top-performing investments will contribute the vast majority of your returns. In fact, it's a common theme among the world's greatest investors that a few winners have carried their entire portfolio. For example, Charlie Munger acknowledges having made almost all his money from a few big winners. The same is true for Benjamin Graham, Peter Lynch, Philip Fisher, Warren Buffett and many other great investors. Typically, they have held these winners for more than a decade, often 20 years or more.

The only time you should consider selling a compounder is when it stops being a great business, the position becomes too large in your portfolio, if the company becomes wildly overpriced or cash is needed to take advantage of a superior opportunity. Otherwise there is no need to reap the gains in compounders as these are companies that increase steadily in value – stocks to 'buy low and let grow'.

Finally, only a handful of your positions need to be winners if you own enough compounders. It is easy to forget, but this is an asymmetric game: you can only lose 1x your investment, but some picks can return 10x or even 100x if you have the confidence and conviction to hold long enough. Although these numbers may seem unfeasible, they are achievable. As Thomas Phelps writes in *100 to 1 in the Stock Market*: "A great many people, I am sure, have never set out to increase their capital one hundredfold because they had no idea that it could be done."

I am sure this is still true today as it was back in 1972, when the book was first published. Moreover, finding one of these 100-baggers might save your whole investment career.

# THE REDEYE TOP PICKS PORTFOLIO

Top Picks is a 'paper trading portfolio' (long only, unhedged) that Redeye offers to private investors who want to learn about investing. The portfolio is based on Redeye's coverage universe of listed Nordic stocks and leverages Redeye's core skills of fundamental research and analysis. Accordingly, we only invest in companies and industries that we already know and understand deeply. After all, true investment risk lies in not knowing what you are doing.

The portfolio's investment approach is highly opportunistic and focused on smaller, less followed growth stocks in the quest for tomorrow's multibaggers – stocks that have prospects for gains of up to 2X and more. This is partly because the small cap space is where an information edge is more likely to be obtained. But the primary advantage of investing in small-cap stocks is that size is the first and foremost differentiator of a multibagger investing approach. It is best summarised by Christopher Mayer in his book *100 Baggers*: "Start with acorns, wind up with oak trees. Start with oak trees, and you won't have quite the same dramatic growth."

We try to identify companies supported by thematic long-term trends – particularly niche market leaders with proven management and a compounding growth outlook. But although we prefer to take a long-term view, we are always ready to act opportunistically if we believe the odds are stacked heavily in our favour. We will come back to this in 'Stocks Fall into Three Buckets' on page 331.

The goal of the disciplined, repeatable investment process is to construct a portfolio of companies with immediate growth potential and the strong likelihood of long-term profitability by the following characteristics: 1) high-quality business; 2) sufficiently undervalued; and 3) the market is about to recognize the full potential of the business. These elements are all different ways to reduce the risk in the stocks we invest in, to provide room for bad luck and mistakes. Below they are described in more detail.

1. **Quality**: Our quality scorecard for companies swings the investment decisions. A company with overall top-level scores of 5 in each category (People, Business, Financials) is typically capable of withstanding the tests of time and adversity. These companies have the potential to improve with time and may be able to generate significant compounding wealth for the long-term owner.

Conversely, no matter the numbers, we refuse to invest in any company that has a People score below 4, as we believe the people behind the company to be the most important thing.

2. **Valuation**: We believe well bought is half sold, which is why we look for businesses that are sufficiently undervalued to warrant an investment. Warren Buffett summarised the point best: "Never count on

making a good sale. Have the purchase price be so attractive that even a mediocre sale gives good results."

The appropriate margin of safety is not static. It may differ across each business that we own based on our degree of uncertainty over its value, which is a function of the quality of the business.

**3. Timeliness.** We believe that cheap alone is not a reason to invest, as this can lead to value traps. We seek to identify a specific path that will allow a company to achieve its full potential in a timely manner, namely catalysts.

Catalysts are ongoing or potential corporate events or a series of events that accelerate value realisation, situations where price and liquidity are likely to increase. They include mergers, tender offers, spin-offs, litigations, regulatory changes, rights offerings, buybacks, activist investor campaigns and many others.

Ideally, in anticipation of a positive catalyst, we want to see sentiment around the stock improving. As stock prices reflect expectations for future financial performance, we always review the stock chart as it will tell us at a glance if we are early on the stock or not. Also, the price trend informs us about market sentiment towards the stock, which is critical to understanding why it may be cheap.

Typically, we see a surge in volume and then in price as we get closer to the catalyst's realisation. This would indicate that investors might be accumulating shares in anticipation of the catalyst playing out. However, a crowded name that has already outperformed based on the expectation of a positive catalyst is likely to get a limited reaction if and when the catalyst does occur.

## TRACK RECORD OF PROVEN RESULTS

<u>Our goal with Top Picks is to compound wealth at a superior rate over the long term, while minimising the risk of permanent losses of capital.</u> We are not trying to be right all the time, but to increase the odds of being right – the hit ratio. Most importantly, we try to make much more money when we are right than we lose when we are wrong – the win-loss ratio.

 Our hit rate over the last five years has been 57%, which means that most of our positions have outperformed the market. This is quite good. As the legendary investor Peter Lynch once pointed out: "In this business, if you're good, you're right six times out of ten."

 However, <u>the real magic in our portfolio is that we have been very good at letting our winners run</u> and become a larger part of our portfolio while selling underperforming stocks before they have had a chance of dragging down the overall performance. Indeed, several of our positions have outperformed the market by several hundred percent over the last five years.

Our win-loss ratio of 523% for the same period is testimony to this. The ratio compares outperformance from good decision-making to alpha lost as a result of poor decisions. In other words, our returns are heavily skewed to the upside. It's all about execution as Lee Freeman-Shor outlines in his great book *The Art of Execution*: "Any poker player knows that it is not how many hands you win that matters, it's how much you win when you win, and how much you lose when you lose."

# THE REDEYE TOP PICKS PORTFOLIO

*Handwritten annotations: "Only half of parts well", "Lo 507 of funds are", "many explain"*

Below you can see the performance for the Redeye Top Picks portfolio, which has returned 436% over the last five years (data as of 15 November 2021), a cumulative annual return of +40%. Very few funds – if any – whose record is public has done anywhere near so well in the period.

TOP PICKS PERFORMANCE VS INDEX (5 YEARS)
15/11 2021: TOP PICKS +436%   OMXSPI +100%

| Source: Redeye Equity Research

Compare our win-loss ratio to the typical mutual fund, where no position is allowed to be larger than 5% of the portfolio. Even if the fund manager finds a compounder, they would fail to back the winner with a sufficient share of their portfolio – to let the winner run its full course and have a significant impact.

A position that grows profitably at 20% a year would soon exceed the 5% position size cap. The fund manager would then be forced to constantly rebalance the portfolio and trim the stock into oblivion. The alternative cost is very high, and the portfolio's pace will be dictated by many of the laggards (the 40th best investment idea rarely outperforms the best). Even though the position would improve the overall performance, it would not turn into a life-changing investment because of the capped upside.

Moreover, consider that many fund managers have a hit rate below 50%. The combination explains why so many struggle to beat the index. Only a few exceptional ones (including Mr. Lynch) have done it consistently over a longer time period.

Our win-loss ratio of 523% explains why our hit rate of 57% is able to generate the outsized returns that we have accomplished over the years. While our hit rate is good, it's our win-loss ratio that knocks the ball out of the park. A general lesson from this is that <u>a few great investments in a portfolio can do wonders if they are retained to let the power of compounding do the work</u>.

Lastly, at Redeye we have successfully invested the company's own funds in line with Top Picks since 2016, with almost no slippage costs. Also, we recently turned the experience and track record of running Top Picks into a fund management business. Since 2020 we have been acting as the sole provider of investment ideas to an alternative investment fund (AIF) – Redeye High-Quality Fund. Today this fund is marketed to a few selected sophisticated investors, friends and family, but clients with short-term mindsets are avoided. As of 29 October 2021, the fund has delivered a gross return before fees of +125% since its inception on 1 May 2020.

## PRINCIPLES OF MANAGING PORTFOLIO RISK

<u>Our protection against risk is primarily in the quality of companies we invest in</u>. That's why our risk management process focuses on ensuring we invest in truly high-quality companies that will continue to grow over the long term. After all, if the business does well, the stock eventually

follows. Moreover, we do not take the scatter-gun approach of holding an excessively large number of stocks. In other words, we try to lower the company specific risk (idiosyncratic risk) in our portfolio by holding high-quality companies to compensate for the higher market risk (systematic risk) that follows with portfolio concentration.

Most mutual funds own anywhere from 50-100 stocks with few exceptions. In almost all cases, this is foolish 'diworsification' and reflects closet indexing rather than prudent money management. Charlie Munger captures this perfectly: "The goal of investments is to find situations where it is safe not to diversify." Munger also said that "a well-diversified portfolio needs just four stocks." Still, <u>diversification is a great concept but, like almost everything else in life, is less good when carried to extremes</u>.

Mutual fund managers often argue that concentrated portfolios are not appropriate for their client base. Generally, people don't have what it takes to weather the occasional high volatility of concentrated portfolios without feeling worries and withdrawing their money. In other words, most mutual funds have a client base that makes the managers incapable of doing a great job. Moreover, most fund managers are judged by their employers based on how they perform against an index or peer group over a short period of time. This all works against concentrating investments in potential long-term winners. As a private investor with no clients or other principals to report to, you don't have those disadvantages. As Philip Fisher has said, "For individuals, any holding of over twenty different stocks is a sign of financial incompetence." The key point is that over-diversified portfolios increase the risk of mediocre returns.

When it comes to diversification, we seek to construct a portfolio that is both highly concentrated but also diverse in terms of sectors, geographic areas, types of value, and between

defensive and cyclical stocks in response to the prevailing stage in the economic cycle. This means that we do not just combine the top ideas of our analysts, but the best combination of ideas. In our case, this means holding around a dozen positions at any time, with the cash position as a diversifier whose size reflects the availability of attractive investment opportunities. Nonetheless, we always try to keep some dry powder for a rainy day.

A highly concentrated portfolio makes it easier for us to stay on top of all of our portfolio holdings to maintain superior understanding of the businesses. Consequently, we have set a minimum position size of 5% to help us concentrate on our best ideas while avoiding more speculative plays. Also, we set the maximum position size at 20% as an insurance policy against over-confidence. Nonetheless, our typical position size is about 5% of the portfolio, with the largest holdings at 15-20% – but only if we have really high confidence and conviction and downside risk is very low. We subscribe to what Joel Greenblatt once said: "My largest positions are not the ones I think I'm going to make the most money from. My largest positions are the ones I don't think I'm going to lose money in."

When we are considering new candidates for the portfolio, we compare each candidate with the most similar stock that we already own – its relative attractiveness. If we have greater confidence and conviction in the new name based on company quality and risk/return trade-off, we will consider selling the existing holding to make room for it. Unfortunately, it's the well-intentioned temptation to jump in and out of investments that too often contributes to bad outcomes. Consequently, a new candidate needs to be significantly more attractive than an existing holding for us to switch the position – something that hardly ever happens if it's a compounder.

Besides selling entire positions, we will often adjust the size of our holdings as our confidence and conviction fluctuates over time. The latter often means that <u>we size our positions over time as we get to know a business better and its track record builds</u>. Also, it can make perfect sense in some situations for us to harvest some gains from a successful investment to put the money to work in a better idea.

We have been fairly good at this over the last seven years, as our portfolio sizing has added value over time. The latter is assessed by comparing the actual cumulative return of the portfolio to that of an equally-weighted portfolio with monthly rebalancing, where the cash position stays the same. All the same, trimming positions is very hard and most investors are probably better off leaving it alone.

## STOCKS FALL INTO THREE BUCKETS

As very few companies compound their equity and earnings at 20% or higher annually for a decade or longer, it's very difficult to compound capital at 20% or more without some turnover in the portfolio. Moreover, truly great compounders are often priced expensively. So achieving above 20% annual returns by buying and holding great businesses for a decade is highly unlikely without selling. High turnover was critical to Warren Buffett generating 50% annual returns in the 1950s, just as it was to Joel Greenblatt doing 40% a year in the 80s and 90s.

This is the main reasons why we are willing to invest opportunistically in <u>deep-value special situations, positions with short-term share price potential</u>, in addition to emerging and long-term compounders. Our investments fit roughly into these three investment opportunities, but the portfolio mix depends on what types of opportunities appear to offer the best risk-adjusted returns at the time.

Below these three opportunities are described in more detail:

### Long-Term Compounders
*Companies with deep moats and long runways*

Long-term, or established, compounders are companies that have durable competitive advantages (also called moats) and attractive internal and external reinvestment opportunities for continued growth, including potential acquisitions. As such, they have long growth runways and demonstrable track records of generating sustainably high returns on capital at annualised returns in the mid-teens or better. Sometimes this includes inorganic growth through buying smaller businesses at bargain prices (so-called serial acquirers or M&A compounders).

Most of the time long-term compounders are too expensive, but they account for the vast majority of the stock market's long-term returns. Trying to invest in these companies purely on an analysis of value is more likely to result in missed opportunities. Similarly, the temptation to rely on spotting the best time to enter a position in a long-term compounder can result in missing the biggest buying opportunities.

In his book *100 to 1 in the Stock Market* Thomas Phelps advocates this stance; "The more successful one is at market timing, the greater is the temptation to rely on it and thus miss much greater opportunities of buying right and holding on." In his study, Phelps found that many stocks could have been bought at 52-week highs for many years and still turn out 100 to one winners. All one has to do is identify them and stick to them.

Consequently, we are ready to invest in long-term compounders at reasonable prices and then remain patient, as the stock performance roughly tracks the return on equity over time. Keep in mind that selling a long-term compounder because of a high valuation often involves hoping to buy back at lower prices later on, which is wishful thinking and not a strategy. Philip Fisher once said, "If the job has been correctly done when a common stock is purchased, the time to sell is almost never."

Long-term compounders are above all high-quality companies. To determine a long-term compounder, at least one of the three categories (People, Business, Financials) in our proprietary company quality rating system must score a 5, while none can score below 4. The key is to assess whether the quality is likely to persist into the future, at least over the next five to 10 years.

When we buy these stocks, we ask ourselves if we would buy the whole company. They might not give explosive returns initially, but hold the potential to be big movers over the long term. Accordingly, we don't regard the short-term performance of a long-term compounder as important as these are likely to be multi-year positions in our portfolio. Instead, we base our decisions for these stocks on the rate of return that we assess an investment will earn over the next three to five years by being highly aware of any optionality in the business. The latter means that the growth outlook is hard to intelligently incorporate in a DCF-model, which explains why we are not too fixated on price.

As Thomas Phelps said, "Perhaps the greatest advantage of all in buying top quality stocks without visible ceilings on their growth is that when we do so we give ourselves the chance to profit by the unforeseeable and incalculable."

In other words, the margin of safety is sufficient if the stock is cheap from a fair value standpoint. This means 15-25% below our Base Case fair value. Anything less demanding amounts to portfolio-filling.

## Emerging Compounders
*Companies with emerging moats*

Most established compounders started their value creation journeys as lesser-known emerging compounders. These companies exhibit quality characteristics today but are often misunderstood. This is generally because they are early in their growth cycle and surging sales have not yet translated to earnings, as they are reinvested for long-term growth.

Emerging compounders are either establishing a new market that is too small to attract competition from larger companies or gaining share in an underpenetrated market, often from a less nimble incumbent. As such, they are often smaller (market cap below EUR 300 m) and managed by executive teams who are progressive and research-minded. Yet, these companies don't usually have a new, cutting edge product – they just have the first version which works, and can be commercialised. Therefore, emerging compounders are typically operating in a growing niche market that is about to take off, in which they have a high market share due to first-mover advantage.

Unlike long-term compounders the resilience of their business model has not been tested across cycles, and it's not yet clear whether incumbents or copycats will be able to catch up as their competitive advantage is still developing. These are often businesses that are about to turn cash flow-positive after years of losses and are poised to grow much faster than the market. In other words, they are typically on the verge of a major breakthrough in sales and market presence. As such, they are perfectly positioned to benefit from high operating leverage as they will see a huge surge in growth, sales, and overall profits in the near future.

On top of that, they are generally not widely owned among institutions as they fall below institutional requirements.

However, they are likely to become both liquid and widely owned by institutions if we turn out to be right about them.

Keep in mind that the greatest gains in a stock are usually made as a business is developing its competitive advantage rather than after it already has developed one. That's why emerging compounders are our investments of choice as long as they are trading in the lower half of the valuation range between our Base and Bear Case Scenarios or below.

In order to catch compounders early in their growth cycle before they experience their big run-ups, we focus more on the trend than immediate performance. Accordingly, to identify emerging compounders, we look for stocks that have a Financials score below 4, while People and Business score 4 or 5 (at least one must score a 5). All the same, companies must have sufficient financing to reach the point of self-sustaining profitability to qualify as an emerging compounder.

Keep in mind that the People score and the Business score are leading indicators that ultimately produce quantitative results in the Financials category. This means that we are spotting something not yet evident in the reported numbers but that should show through over time. As a result, we might find these investments at cheap levels, but it still takes a lot of vision and imagination to find them early. Obviously, it's much harder to know which companies will be the high-quality growers of the future than to simply screen for which companies were great in the past.

## Deep-Value Special Situations
*Cheap stocks with tangible trigger events*

These investment opportunities include both average quality companies whose stock prices are suffering from a negative short-term event, and also overlooked or misunderstood companies that are about to be discovered but are still available at a deep discount. It is about taking advantage of market over-reactions or exploitation of overly conservative expectations, <u>situations where stocks are about to enjoy a rerating</u>.

The return potential and risk level in these opportunities are both above average but they offer asymmetric payoffs. Needless to say, <u>with deep-value special situations, we spend more time on the downside case than the business model and the sustainability of returns</u>. Keep in mind that current earnings usually have little to do with the long-term earnings power that we envision in these companies. However, deep-value special situations have low correlation with other investments and are less sensitive to the vagaries of the business and macroeconomics due to their short duration.

<u>The cornerstone in special situations is the confidence in potential near-term catalysts</u> and the market forces of reversion to the mean to drive the stock to its fair value and generate a decent return. What we are looking for is attractive risk-adjusted returns with an expected quick pay-off. Besides potential catalysts, these stocks must be bought with a large margin of safety – especially as they are bought to be sold to someone else at a higher price in the near future.

For a catalyst to be valid, there must be solid arguments for both why the value of a stock should be able to rise and when the event is to occur. When strong catalysts are nowhere to be found, it can be useful to remember that companies are often rightly cheap, so-called 'value traps'.

The ideal time to act is usually directly before, during and right after the catalyst event – just before the stock price might surge. Hence, the window of opportunity is typically open for a short time only and therefore the holding period may also be short, translating into high annual returns.

We are well aware of being too far ahead of the market is very similar to being wrong. For an investment in a deep-value special situation stock to be warranted, we emphasize a tangible trigger event within the next six months, sufficient liquidity and a price level close to our most pessimistic outlook (i.e., our Bear Case fair value). Also, we typically decline to invest in deep-value special situations with a People score below 4 (a minimum acceptable quality) in our proprietary company quality rating system, as it reduces the risk of a 'value trap'.

Finally, a complementary key factor is whether the major shareholders have recently been buyers or sellers. If either, they have almost certainly done good homework and we should pay attention.

## SEVEN CONSIDERATIONS BEFORE INVESTING

In the Top Picks portfolio's investment committee we use a set of questions that seem to be helpful in organizing thoughts and prioritizing opportunities to achieve attractive investment results. These remind us that intelligent investing is just as much about risk as it is about returns.

Typically, the more illiquid a stock is, the more difficult and expensive it is to trade. Accordingly, we want most of our holdings to be relatively liquid. This gives us a 'right to change our mind' and exit a position, either because our analysis was wrong or because new facts or better ideas emerge. Therefore, we always want to reassure ourselves on the liquidity front by asking: "Is the stock liquid enough?".

Typically, we never want to buy a stock if our target position is larger than half the average daily trading volume, as it would take about a week (five trading days) to buy or sell a full position. The latter assumes that we can trade up to 10% of the average daily trading volumes without moving the stock price. However, the bar is set higher for deep-value special situations, as we must be able to sell the whole position in a day on minimal down-ticks, if necessary.

To make good investing decisions, we always try to look for reasons not to buy the stock. If we're losing sleep over an investment, it's simply not worth it. That is why we always start out by asking two very basic questions: "<u>What could go wrong?</u>" and "<u>What is the floor price for the stock?</u>".

These questions force us to think about the fact that we are buying a business and not just speculating on an increase in its stock price. If the answers to these two questions suggest an absolute downside of more than 50% in a prevailing bull market, we typically want to pass on the investment. We never want to buy a stock that can't come back after a big drop. Basically, this helps us avoid big mistakes by being aware of that we are wrong about 40% of the time.

The next question is another basic one, but again it is surprisingly helpful: "<u>Will this stock double over the next two years?</u>". This question allows us to dismiss less compelling opportunities and focus on the high-conviction best ideas. However, for a deep-value special situation stock to be a worthy investment this question translates into the question of whether the stock can be expected to achieve an annualised return of at least 50%. This extra margin of safety is due to the inherent risk of a delayed catalyst that is associated with event-driven investments.

A good complementary question is: "<u>What are the market's current assumptions for the stock?</u>" This question is assessed by reviewing the stock chart, consensus estimates, and how the stock is priced in relation to our fair value range and its peers, as well as in a historical context.

Another great complementary question we ask ourselves is: "<u>Where are we thinking differently from the market?</u>". This question is important because the most successful ideas are generally where we have a non-consensual view. This is especially important when it comes to deep-value special situations, as we only invest in these when the opportunity becomes irresistible from a contrarian standpoint. This often happens when companies undergo significant change, but requires being sceptical and in a good position to take advantage of the herd's mistakes. It also includes being aware of the tendency for mid and small caps to outperform when they are at a significant discount (at least 20%) to large-cap valuations.

The final question we ask in order to be prepared to invest is: "Will this company be a good fit with the existing portfolio?". It is asked in an attempt to reduce risk and increase returns through diversification.

Lastly, when a stock that we own drops, we recheck all the facts and seek to understand what caused the fall. If we believe the company is not as strong as we initially thought, we sell the investment rather than trying to find a new reason for owning the stock at a lower price point. It allows us to get out of the stock before the loss grows bigger. But if we believe the decline is temporary, and the investment is still poised for success, we find the courage to buy more or sit tight. Nonetheless, we always prefer to average up and buy more shares at a higher price when the company fundamentals develop in the right direction and better than expected.

# CLOSING WORDS

## EXPERIENCE IS THE BEST TEACHER

As with most important and interesting things in life, investing is a constant learning exercise. If you try to learn every day your insights and conclusions will never be final. There is simply no end to what you can learn, particularly from the best investors' hard-earned experience. Committing a great deal of time to read and learn from the great investors' mistakes and successes is necessary for your own eventual success. Mark Twain once quipped that "the man who doesn't read good books has no advantage over the man who cannot read them."

As you try to learn from other investors, keep in mind that you are the product of the people you hang around, so choose them wisely. Cultivate people in your life that make you better. The people you are near tend to have a much more profound effect on your behaviour than you think, as we typically adopt the behaviour of those around us. Still, to evolve as an investor, you should be open to different ways of looking at investing as there are many ways of succeeding.

Another way to learn is to take dry runs by using dummy portfolios ('paper trading') in which you make trades that simulate real positions. A further one is to go to investing schools to learn how it works in theory. A less common way is to teach. And still another one is to write articles as a way of thinking more clearly and building deeper understanding. Writing this book has been a tremendous learning experience for me.

The key is to go to bed a little wiser each night. Learning tends to make you more curious – the more you know, the more you want to know. Nonetheless, simulation, textbook theory and writing are no substitutes for investing, since most mistakes in investing are emotional or psychological. We all have inherent biases that influence our investment decisions. These can be suppressed by building a deep knowledge of the business behind the stock, but only to some extent.

At some point the only way to refine your skills is to commit real money. Where the rubber meets the road is when you actually make an investment and manage that position over your investing timeframe. Until you study the real world in real time with real money you haven't put yourself in a place where your ability to master your emotions is tested. As Peter Lynch says, "It isn't the head but the stomach that determines the fate of the stock picker".

Experience counts. As good judgement comes from experience, and experience comes from bad judgment, the most successful investors learn by doing – not just studying. The lessons that really stick are the ones we stumbled across ourselves.

Trial and error is the best way of moving forward, and failure is the road to success. Accordingly, focus on process more than outcome to learn from your mistakes. Keep a journal and review your investment decisions after the outcomes are known, and you will start to see what works for you and what doesn't. Gradually you will improve your investment process and end up making fewer mistakes. A good process will be followed by good results over time.

For example, as I've grown as an investor, so too have my average time horizon and performance. What I've learned is you can make much more just by having a slightly longer time horizon with your investments. For this to work you need to develop a high boredom threshold and not easily being drawn into new ideas. There is an old saying: "Your portfolio is like a bar of soap, the more you handle it, the smaller it gets." Moreover, you must view investing as a means to produce wealth instead of income, by not focusing on your short-term desires. Keep in mind that wealth is what you accumulate, not what you spend.

The nature of compounding might give you the impression that getting an early entry is the only way to benefit from it. But even if you catch the compounding train late, it can still get you to your destination as long as you avoid catastrophic mistakes. Identifying and investing in high-quality businesses with multibagger potential is a great way of trying to reduce these mistakes.

Finally, the richest person in the world isn't the person with most money, but the person that spent the most time with the ones they loved.

*I hope you found the book enjoyable, educational and profitable. I'd love your thoughts on it, either in a review on Amazon or in a direct email to me: bjorn@redeye.se*

Björn Fahlén
November 15$^{th}$, 2021

# APPENDIX A: CHANNEL CHECKS

## TALKING TO PEOPLE AROUND THE BUSINESS

Developing the expertise in recognising investment opportunities requires continued monitoring of companies, something which can be facilitated by building durable relationships with people who are close to the company or more knowledgeable about its industry than you. In this way, you are better placed to analyse companies' long-term trajectories and their many potential twists and turns along the way.

This long view based on field research is a major advantage to delivering long-term performance. Yet many investors, even professionals, only conduct superficial due diligence on companies by analysing readily available information like corporate presentations, financial statements, and press releases. However, this type of research will only show you part of the story.

After all, management often suffers from over-optimism about their business or, worse, is misleading about it. You can never be sure you are getting the full story. After all, they won't usually say the stock is ahead of events – telling you to sell.

Known as 'channel checks', this field research approach is an effective route to distinguishing yourself with modest effort. It provides insight unavailable from purely public information such as financial statements, management presentations, or other standard industry releases. It's all about gathering small pieces of non-material information and piecing them together to form a material conclusion.

Ensure you do your channel checks and use any contacts you have. These could be its customers, competitors, suppliers, current or former employees, or industry experts. Make it a routine to check whether conventional wisdom has empirical support by asking intelligent questions to these people.

For example, you could use LinkedIn to look up suppliers, partners, current and former employees (make sure they left on friendly terms). Contact them via email and ask if they're willing to speak with you for a few minutes. In exchange, you can explain how investors view their industry.

Another great source of insight is to ask industry experts and competitors where and why they would invest if they had money to spend (excluding their own company in the case of competitors). Doing this, you can quickly form a picture of who is best. At the very least you will usually hear some interesting answers and reasons for them.

Also, it helps to think like a consumer and, if possible, sign up for a sales call as a potential customer. Similarly, make use of sources like Reddit, Twitter or Glassdoor.

The legendary investor Philip Fisher called this type of information 'Scuttlebutt'. "It is amazing what an accurate picture of the relative points of strength and weakness of each company in an industry can be obtained from a representative cross-section of the opinions of those who in one way or another are concerned with any particular company. Most people, particularly if they feel sure there is no danger of their being quoted, like to talk rather freely about their competitors. Go to five companies in an industry, ask each of them intelligent questions about the points of strength and weakness of the other four, and nine times out of ten a surprisingly detailed and accurate picture of all five will emerge," he says.

Fisher goes on to say that an investor must make it clear beyond doubt that the source of the information will never be revealed. The investor must live up to this or run the risk of not having opinions passed along. When using the scuttlebutt approach, it is best to diversify your sources and cross-check any information that is obtained. This to check the reliability and legitimacy, for limitations such as prejudice, bias and hidden incentives.

For example, if you think there is an issue with competition for a particular product you can go through many different distributors, such as stores or shops, and see if the product is positioned the way management suggests.

NOTE: The word scuttlebutt originally referred to a barrel used to store drinking water on sailing ships. 'Butt' referred to the barrel and 'scuttle' meant to chop or drill a hole as for tapping a cask. Sailors would gather around the scuttlebutt to drink water and, as they did, they exchanged gossip – just the way people in offices do today over coffee or tea. Eventually, the term scuttlebutt came to refer not just to the barrel, but also to the rumours and gossip.

# HOW TO CONDUCT YOUR CHANNEL CHECKS

Channel checks are a common way of conducting primary research. It is typically performed after initial financial analysis. A few simple guidelines:

**Identify your mission and develop a clear hypothesis:** It is very easy to finish a conversation with little new information due to a lack of planning and research. It's important to make it very clear to yourself which two or three questions you really want to get answered. What part of the investment decision do you need to get comfortable with? It's important to know where you want to go and what kind of uncertainties you wish to reduce or eliminate. Use the checklist provided in this book to find out.

Typically, by interviewing the management first you will get answers that make for good conversation material when you talk with other sources. The goal with interviewing the management is primarily to develop a deeper understanding of the business and its strategy.

**Understand the business and its industry:** If you aren't knowledgeable about the business and its industry, you won't be able to ask proper questions and interpret the answers you are given. People find you out very easily when you are unprepared or unqualified to speak about a segment or industry. Since they are looking to exchange ideas and information, you will squander the opportunity if you are unprepared. Your counter party will be less likely to give you information if they feel you cannot help them in return – to deliver any value. Keep in mind that the best way to become successful is to deserve it.

**Ask for a follow-up**: Be direct and ask for a follow-up. It is always beneficial to build relationships with professionals in the industries you are interested in. It may help you identify new trends.

**Be appreciative**: Be extremely gracious and considerate when speaking to industry contacts and tell each person how helpful the conversation was. Compliment them on their knowledge. This will help you maintain and develop relationships and improve your response rate.

## WHAT TO EXPECT

**Expect to get called out:** It's inevitable. People will eventually realize that you are not an industry participant but an analyst or investor, and they may call you out on this. Do not overreact and hang up – simply try to level with them. Honesty is the best way to go.

**Expect only 15-20% of the people you contact to talk to you:** The friendlier you are, the better the call will go. However, most people you might want to contact will be busy, or may know that you are an analyst or investor, and may not speak to you as a result.

**In-person contacts are the most effective:** In-person meetings are more intimate than phone conversations and are very helpful in developing relationships.

**Try to identify a consistent theme:** If you hear the same trend mentioned three times or more, you may have uncovered something – especially if it is not broadly known.

## WHAT TO DO

- Write down all your questions first and then edit your list. If you have too many questions, it will be very difficult to accomplish anything. Test your list out on friends or colleagues to make sure your questions are logical and flow well.

- Think about how to introduce yourself in order to lighten up the conversation and make the other person feel comfortable. Make the first impression a positive one. Always show up with a smile on your face to get your source in a positive frame of mind. Try to warmly compliment their unique abilities and make them feel that you value them. But any compliments must be genuine or they will backfire on you. However, the more comfortable someone is, the more they will be willing to share.

- Slow it down, don't jump from question to question. Always pause and let a question sink in. Don't worry as the other person will fill the silence. If you are too much in a hurry, people can feel as if you are not interested about what they have to say.

- Let the other people do the talking and do not interrupt them. Once they know you are listening, they may tell you something valuable.

  If you want them to be more detailed, use mirroring by repeating the last three words they just said – or the most critical one of them. After this you must be silent for at least four seconds to let the mirror work its magic. Mirroring is the art of insinuating similarity, which facilitates bonding and trust.

- Consider words, tone, and body language and try to spot changes and look for incongruities.

- Make sure you are spending time talking to the right people. The information is only as good as the source.

For example, when talking to former employees, make sure there aren't any conflict of interest or issues with contractual obligations. Also, for their understanding to be up to date they must typically have left the company within the last 18 months.

- Always write up a summary of your notes. This will help you re-process all the information and provide a helpful record of all of your discussions.

## QUESTIONS TO ASK

- People are most comfortable talking about themselves or providing their own thoughts. Let the source open up by asking for their opinions instead of directly asking for the facts.

- In general, strive to ask open-ended, probing questions that do not favour a specific view or guide a conversation overly. Let the dialogue develop, it is acceptable to go slightly off-topic or change the order. But don't be afraid to interrupt if you feel the source is not answering your questions. Sometimes, as an alternative to asking open-ended questions, it can work to make a specific statement and ask for his or her view on it.

- Ask questions involving comparisons. This will help you identify trends and establish helpful reference points.

- Instead of asking about specific financial targets it's better to ask how the company is going to reach those targets. But if you must use numbers, use ranges. The risk that the source would be handing over material inside information increases significantly if you ask for quantitative data rather than more qualitative information.

- Always ask the people you want to survey if any confidentiality agreement prohibits them from speaking with you about the topic. The risk of an employee breaching a duty of confidentiality is lower if they are surveyed about competitors, suppliers or distributors, or about other companies´ products.

# APPENDIX B: DISCOUNT RATE

## WHAT IS A DISCOUNT RATE

As an investor, the discount rate serves as a yardstick for your required rate of return. Put simply, it represents the return you require for taking on the risk of owning the stock. A stable, predictable company will have a low required rate, while a risky company with unpredictable cash flows will have a higher required rate.

This is one aspect of incorporating business quality into your margin of safety. After all, quality – like growth – is part of valuation. Nonetheless, it's not the formula that matters most, but the reliability of the cash flows.

Risky companies can be characterised by volatile financial results, unproven business model, untrustworthy management, and/or limited operating history – any of which can lead to wide margins of error in earnings growth and intrinsic value.

Yet you can never fully compensate for risk by using a high discount rate. At some point the risk is not worth taking, no matter how cheap the company may seem. This is why quality trumps valuation in successful investing.

# ESTIMATING THE DISCOUNT RATE

At Redeye, we primarily assess company value by discounting future cash flows (see 'Redeye's Valuation Approach' on page 365). Discounted cash flow forecasts are highly sensitive. A change of just a few basis points in the discount rate can have a big impact on the final figure.

For this reason, it is essential to use an appropriate and conservative figure that reflects both the investment risk and the current interest rate environment.

The discount rate is a key assumption in any Discounted Cash Flow (DCF) model. But there is no precise way of calculating the exact discount rate that you should use. While much material on discount rates is available, we use a simplified approach for practical purposes.

The rate we use at Redeye to discount cash flows is a company's Weighted Average Cost of Capital (WACC). This derives from our use of the 'cash flow to the firm' method.

A company's WACC accounts for both its cost of equity and its cost of debt. The relative weights attached to debt and equity are based on the proportions of each that the company targets for its capital structure over the long term. Here's the basic formula for WACC:

*Weighted Cost of Capital = (Weight of Debt) \* (Cost of Debt \* (1-Tax Rate)) + (Weight of Equity) \* (Cost of Equity)*

The tax rate adjustment on the cost of debt incorporates the tax benefit of the deductibility of interest expenses.

## COST OF EQUITY

A company's cost of equity (COE) represents the average, annualized, nominal total return expected by shareholders. For most companies, COE is the dominant factor in the company's WACC and therefore holds sizable influence in the valuation process. However, the COE presents a significant challenge because it is unobservable in the marketplace.

The most common methodology for estimating COE is the Capital Asset Pricing Model (CAPM). However, there is significant disagreement over appropriate values for the equity risk premium and beta. For this reason, we use a simplified COE methodology that captures the logic of the CAPM while we take a largely qualitative and forward-looking approach. Our goal is to provide reasonable distinctions between the risk characteristics and expected returns of different companies while minimizing the effects of recency bias, false precision, and market noise.

We use a build-up approach to derive COE estimates for individual companies:

**Equity Risk Premium** = Market Average Real Return Expectation. We use 6.0%, based on what we observe as a mean-reverting real return (inflation adjusted) of the Swedish stock market over long rolling time horizons – this is not a forecast, but rather what we believe shapes investor expectations.

**+Risk-Free Rate**

We use the average yield of the 10-year bond over the past decade, as a proxy for the normalised long-term risk-free rate. At the time of writing this stands at 1.0%.

**+Company-Specific Risk Premium**

This is based on our assessment of the predictability of the company's future cash flows. While it is easier to forecast those of high-quality companies, we use the company's quality rating as a proxy for the company-specific risk premium; ranges from -1.0% to +10.0%).

In practice, the company-specific risk premium is derived by aggregating all 19 sub-category scores from our company quality rating model, as follows:

| AGGREGATED SUB-CATEGORY SCORE | COMPANY-SPECIFIC RISK PREMIUM |
|---|---|
| 78-90 | -1.0% |
| 67-77 | — |
| 58-66 | 1.0% |
| 51-57 | 2.0% |
| 45-50 | 3.0% |
| 40-44 | 4.0% |
| 36-39 | 5.0% |
| 33-35 | 6.0% |
| 30-32 | 8.0% |
| 0-29 | 10.0% |

Source: Redeye Equity Research

## COST OF DEBT

The cost of debt is the return that a company provides to its debtholders and creditors – the cost of raising financing. Since observable interest rates play a big role in quantifying the cost of debt, it is relatively more straightforward to calculate the cost of debt than the cost of equity.

In estimating the cost of debt, we look at its current or implied credit rating and comparable debts to estimate its cost of debt. If the company doesn't have a bond or credit rating, we would evaluate the default risk of the company and its leverage ratios, in particular, its interest coverage ratio. Also, when comparing with other companies within the same industry, the capital structure of the company should be in line with its peers.

EXAMPLE

A company has the following scores for their sub-categories in our company quality rating model:

| PEOPLE SCORE | | BUSINESS SCORE | | FINANCIALS SCORE | |
| --- | --- | --- | --- | --- | --- |
| 5 | BUSINESS PASSION | 5 | BUSINESS SCALABILITY | 4 | EARNINGS POWER |
| 5 | EXECUTION CAPABILITY | 3 | MARKET STRUCTURE | 4 | PROFIT MARGIN |
| 5 | CAPITAL ALLOCATION | 3 | VALUE PROPOSITION | 4 | GROWTH RATE |
| 5 | INVESTOR COMMUNICATION | 3 | COMPETITIVE MOAT | 3 | FINANCIAL HEALTH |
| 5 | EXECUTIVE COMPENSATION | 4 | OPERATIONAL RISKS | 5 | EARNINGS QUALITY |
| 4 | OWNERSHIP STRENGTH | 2 | SOCIAL RESPONSIBILITY | | |
| 3 | BOARD LEADERSHIP | | | | |

AGGREGATED SUB-CATEGORY SCORE     **72**

# ESTIMATING THE DISCOUNT RATE

An aggregated sub-category score of 72 translates into a company-specific risk premium of 0%. Adding a 1.0% Risk-Free Rate and a 6.0% in equity risk premium brings the cost of equity of 7.0%.

Now we can calculate the WACC. As the market value of the company's equity is EUR 600 m and it has EUR 400 m of debt on its balance sheet, 60% of its capital is equity and 40% is debt. With its cost of equity at 7.0% and its cost of debt at 4%, its WACC is:

$$(60\% \times 7.0\%) + (40\% \times 4\% *(1-0.22)) = 5.5\%$$

# APPENDIX C: VALUATION

## DEALING WITH UNCERTAINTY

The best estimate of a company's intrinsic value is the discounted net present value of all anticipated but inevitably uncertain future cash flows that will accrue to investors from the company's operations. At Redeye, we use a Discounted Cash Flow (DCF) model to discount these back to current value at a rate that reflects their risk and uncertainty.

The primary goal of employing this model isn't to determine a definite value, but rather to understand uncertainty about value. Because humans tend to anchor too readily to a single outcome or frame decisions too narrowly, we always try to think about several possible outcomes, or scenarios, rather than just one. After all, stocks don't trade at one point over any extended period of time. We label these scenarios our Bull, Base and Bear cases.

To understand exactly what underlies the differences between scenarios we try to dig into the key value drivers that account for the major disparities in valuation. While many factors contribute, a few variables always weigh most heavily. When you know the company, it's relatively easy to figure these out. They may include its potential market size, its profit margins, its market penetration or other critical variables.

By linking our scenario analysis to key value drivers, we aim to provide better understanding of the sources of both value creation and downside risks. This should enable better-informed, more objective investment decisions.

The differences in valuation between our different scenarios simply underscore uncertainty around the company's value, as shown in the graphic below.

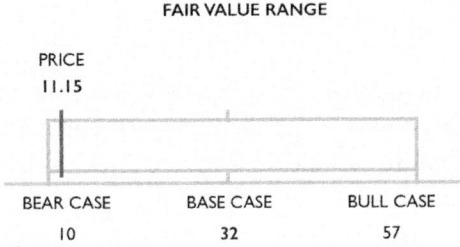

Source: Redeye Equity Research

When it comes to probabilities, we always try to think like statisticians in generating an unbiased baseline prediction. We may also adjust the baseline in light of specific information about the case, but only if there are particular reasons to expect the optimistic bias to be more or less pronounced than in similar cases.

# REDEYE'S VALUATION APPROACH

At Redeye we have divided the forecast period in our financial models into three stages. This contrasts with traditional two-stage DCF models:

- Stage 1: The 'explicit forecast period' is the detailed cash flow period

- Stage 2: We assume excess returns are eroded by competition

- Stage 3: All excess returns have been eliminated and ROIC equals WACC

One of the model's most important assumptions is earnings for the last year of Stage 1 as these serve as the jumping-off point for all future years. This last year typically falls within the next 10 years and should represent a mid-cycle year to avoid basing Stages 2 and 3 on a cyclical peak or trough. Accordingly, great care should always be taken over its calculation.

The length of Stage 2 depends on how quickly excess returns are exhausted. This in turn depends on the business's defensibility and exposure to structural growth drivers. Strong sustainable competitive advantages in combination with secular growth trends, long product cycles and optionality to develop additional avenues of growth for entry into other markets can make this stage last more than 20 years. Yet it typically lasts no more than five years for average companies that lack economic moats.

Beyond this growth period of diminishing returns on invested capital, a terminal value is applied to cash flows. This is the Stage 3 period and its growth rate will be in line with GDP growth at best as we assume competition eliminates all excess returns.

In addition to our cash flow-based analysis we often use a comparables approach to make snapshot comparisons with industry peers and/or to measure value (price) versus sector or market averages. This provides a 'quick and dirty' indication of relative value measured against how much investors are willing to pay for similar companies today.

Yet price and value are two very distinct concepts. So this valuation method should be treated with some degree of scepticism. However, for an investment case based on a catalyst with a timeframe shorter than 12 months, a comparables approach might be more useful than a DCF model for establishing a valuation that reflects short-term market sentiment. After all, our fair values are meant to provide a range estimate of what the stock is worth, not target prices or what investors are willing to pay for it.

Even so, a DCF model is useful both for more accurate fundamental valuation and for 'reverse engineering' valuation estimates based on multiples models and/or subjective judgements like the growth rate implicit in the share price.

## BULL, BASE AND BEAR SCENARIOS

At Redeye we assess risk/reward by determining what we think a company is worth today (Base Case), what it could be worth on the upside if management executes its business plan successfully (Bull Case), and what could go wrong with our Base Case – the downside if the company stumbles (Bear Case). The key here is to allow for outliers by focusing on the range of possible outcomes, from upside to downside scenarios, rather than a single most likely scenario.

"Plans are best-case scenarios. Let's avoid anchoring on plans when we forecast actual outcomes. Thinking about ways the plan could go wrong is one way to do it," as Daniel Kahneman once explained this. The bottom line is: if you are going to make errors, at least cover your tail.

At Redeye, we are highly conscious of what could go wrong, not what the discount is to fair value. We argue that a reasonable margin of safety depends on the quality of the business, differentiating between the stocks we own primarily because of price and those we own because of a high affinity for the business.

For the former category a reasonable margin of safety is achieved when a stock is purchased at a price below or at our Bear Case fair value. But for long-term compounders we are ready to invest at a small discount to our Base Case fair value.

So the Base Case and Bear Case are great reference points for buyers, whether the stock is a potential compounder or more of a value play. In the end, of course, our fair value estimates are more of a guide than automatic buy or sell prices.

Looking closely at the Bear Case scenario will certainly help you to have a more balanced view than just focusing on the potential upside in the Bull Case scenario. Moreover, at least some of the confirmation bias in analysts' models can be eliminated by forecasting scenarios.

Accordingly, Redeye's concept of valuation range enables confidence and conviction buying when everyone else is selling, and maintaining positions that are at odds with popular opinion. All the same, any Bear Case scenario is often more consequential to the stock price than the forecast itself.

**The Bear Case** should answer the question:

*Why might someone prefer to be a seller of the stock?*

It should include the following (in 6-10 bullet points): Our conservative Key Model Assumptions that drive value if controversy turns out to be permanent (including the discount rate), i.e. what could go wrong and has to happen for the downside case to play out? If that event plays out, what will happen to the valuation or how large is the downside risk? What is our subjective likelihood of the downside scenario and what is the likely potential loss?

The Bull Case serves investment discipline by identifying a potential exit, particularly if it's a business you own primarily because of its quality. The key here is genuine long-term thinking and being patient enough to hold good investments until the market recognises their full potential. Once a position is taken, the Bull Case will help to avoid premature selling. Just because prices are not attractive enough to buy is not a reason to sell. However, a position in a company should be sold entirely when the share price reflects the Bull Case (or when cash is needed to take advantage of a superior opportunity elsewhere). In practice, if it's a company of average quality, the stock is best sold at the Base Case fair value when the temporary conditions that led to the mispricing have passed.

**The Bull Case** should answer the question:

*What would a blue-sky scenario look like?*

It should include the following (in 6-10 bullet points): Our conservative Key Model Assumptions that drive value if things go better than expected (including the discount rate), i.e. what has to happen for the upside case to play out? If that event plays out, what will happen to the valuation or how large is the upside potential? What is our subjective likelihood of an upside event and what is the likely potential gain?

# APPENDIX D: QUALITY CHECKLIST

# PEOPLE
## DOES THE COMPANY HAVE GREAT PEOPLE BEHIND IT?

**Is the CEO passionate about the business opportunity?**

1. Does the CEO have a visionary attitude towards the business's opportunities?
2. Does the CEO think independently and exhibit original ideas?
3. Does the CEO have strong market insight?
4. Has the CEO stayed in the same industry for more than a decade?
5. Does the CEO show genuine excitement for their products?
6. *Does the CEO serve on a significant number of outside boards?*

**Does management appear to have strong execution capabilities?**

1. Does management have complementary skills and relevant sector experience?
2. Have the senior team and CEO been together for more than five years?
3. Is there a sound strategy for long-term growth?
4. Does management tend to deliver on promises, on time and according to plan?
5. Has the CEO done it successfully before?
6. *Does the CEO face personal challenges that might cloud his or her judgement?*

### Does management appear to use shareholders money well?

1. Do the company's incentive plans encourage long-term value creation?
2. Do investments and acquisitions focus on strengthening the core business?
3. Is there consistency in the people responsible for capital allocation?
4. Has the company taken opportunistic action over an attractively priced stock?
5. Have total shares in issue remained constant or decreased over time?
6. *Does the company lack a sound dividend payout policy?*

**Is communication with shareholders open and honest?**

1. Is management sincere and upfront about the business's difficulties and mistakes?
2. Does the CEO uphold company values and link them to its success?
3. Is management's communication timely and clear?
4. Does management consistently use the same 'story' and key metrics?
5. Is communication focused on long-term business value?
6. *Is management's responsiveness to inquiries poor?*

**Does the company have reasonable levels of executive pay?**

1. Does the CEO's pay appear reasonable for a company of this size and profit level?
2. Does the company disclose bonus measures and targets?
3. Does the CEO's pay appear to be in line with other executives?
4. Do the CEO's exit payments appear reasonable?
5. Is the company free of any abuse of options or equity-based incentives?
6. *Does the CEO's pay exceed performance relative to peers?*

**Does the company have strong and capable ownership?**

1. Does the company have a large outside shareholder on the board?
2. Does the management team own a significant stake in the business?
3. Does the company have a controlling owner with long-term ambitions?
4. Is the founder still involved in the business?
5. Are the principal shareholders' interests aligned with those of minority shareholders?
6. *Does the company have classes of stock with different voting rights?*

**Does the board of directors appear to be objective and effective?**

1. Is a majority of the board composed of genuinely independent directors?
2. Does the board hold regular meetings without the CEO to review his or her performance?
3. Is the size of the board reasonable?
4. Do most board directors appear business-savvy and shareholder-oriented?
5. Is the company free of abuses of power for personal gain?
6. *Does the chairman serve on an excessive number of outside boards?*

# BUSINESS

DOES THE BUSINESS HAVE
FAVOURABLE LONG-TERM
PROSPECTS?

**Is the business model repeatable and scalable?**

1. Are a major portion of existing or potential revenues recurring?
2. Does the company have strategic alliances that can help drive its total sales?
3. Is the business asset-light and able to scale up without expensive reinvestment?
4. Is strategy focused on organic growth?
5. Does the company have a history of successful expansion into new markets or locations?
6. *Is this a pre-revenue company which hasn't yet proven its business model?*

**Does the business operate in a favourable market structure?**

1. Does the business have a long runway for growth?
2. Does the business operate in a highly profitable industry?
3. Does the business operate in a slow-changing market with long product cycles?
4. Does the business have limited competition?
5. Is the business resilient in the face of new innovations?
6. *Does the company make an exciting product or operate in a sexy industry?*

## Do the products provide unique and desired benefits to customers?

1. Does the company have a focused core group of customers?
2. Do the products solve a genuine customer need, rather than create desire?
3. Are the products only modestly vulnerable to substitutes?
4. Does the company offer good value to its customers?
5. Does the development process take place in close co-operation with paying customers?
6. *Is constant heavy spending on marketing required for growth?*

## Is this a defensible business that can stay competitive?

1. Does the company enjoy market leadership?
2. Is the company's competitive position strengthening?
3. Do the company's returns on capital consistently exceed its cost of capital?
4. Does the business have a competitive moat that is easy to identify?
5. Does the company possess the ability to raise prices without losing customers?
6. *Has the gross profit margin declined over the past three years?*

**Does the business have limited exposure to significant operational risks?**

1. Does the business have a wide revenue base?
2. Are the business's earnings largely unaffected by commodity prices?
3. Is the business relatively immune to regulatory risk?
4. Is the business independent of any major partners?
5. Is the business defensive and independent of market conditions?
6. *Does the business depend on key employees for its future success?*

**Does the business operate in a socially and environmentally responsible way?**

1. Are the products for the greater good?
2. Has the company avoided sustainability-related incidents over the past five years?
3. Does the company have a purpose-driven leadership?
4. Do employees enjoy working for the company?
5. Are sustainability indicators incorporated into the incentive system?
6. *Does the company lack disclosure on environmental and social issues?*

# FINANCIALS

## DOES THE BUSINESS HAVE SOLID FINANCIAL FUNDAMENTALS?

**Does the company have strong earnings capacity?**

1. Has Return on Assets (ROA) been consistently above the industry average?
2. Is Return on Equity (ROE) higher than 10%?
3. Has Return on Equity (ROE) increased over the past three years?
4. Is average Return on Equity (ROE) at least 20% for the past five years?
5. Has Return on Equity (ROE) been consistent over the past seven years?
6. *Does Return on Equity (ROE) appear unsustainably high?*

## Has the company generated high and consistent profit margins?

NON-FINANCIAL COMPANIES

1. Is Gross Profit Margin higher than 50%?
2. Is operating margin (EBIT) above industry average?
3. Has the average operating margin (EBIT) been higher than 15% for the past three years?
4. Has operating margin (EBIT) increased for three years in a row?
5. Has Net Profit Margin been positive in the past 10 years?
6. *Does the company have high operating leverage?*

*Financial Companies (replacement questions)*

1. Is Net Interest Margin (NIM) above the industry average?
2. Is the Efficiency Ratio below 60%?

## Does the company have a strong growth trend?

1. Is the annual Retention Ratio above 70%?
2. Has annual growth rate in revenue been consistently above the industry average?
3. Is the annual growth rate in revenue above 15%?
4. Is annual growth in earnings (EPS) above 15%?
5. Have earnings (EPS) increased in each of the past five years?
6. *Have earnings (EPS) grown at an extreme rate over the last three years?*

## Is the company in good financial condition?

NON-FINANCIAL COMPANIES

1. Are Current Assets 1.5 times greater than Current Liabilities?
2. Is Total Debt less than three times the Operating Cash Flow?
3. Is Total Debt less than 10 times Free Cash Flow?
4. Is the Debt to Equity ratio below 50%?
5. Is interest on debt covered more than five times by earnings (EBIT)?
6. *Does the company underspend on maintaining its assets?*

LOSS-MAKING NON-FINANCIAL COMPANIES (REPLACEMENT QUESTIONS)

4. Do cash and short-term investments cover expected cash burn (negative Free Cash Flow) for more than two years?
5. Is the company likely to become sustainably cash flow-positive this or next year?
6. Does the company need to raise cash in the capital markets within 12 months?

FINANCIAL INSTITUTIONS (REPLACEMENT QUESTIONS)

1. Is Leverage (Assets to Equity) less than 15 times?
2. Is the Common Equity Tier 1 (CET1) ratio above 10%?
3. Does the institution have a strong Texas ratio?
4. Is Non-Performing Loan exposure less than 2%?
5. Have Net Charge-Offs been consistently lower than peers'?
6. *Has deposit growth stagnated or declined over the past three years?*

**Is the quality of the company's earnings high?**

1. Does the company manage its inventory well?
2. Does the company manage its credit sales well?
3. Are one-time adjustments to earnings rare?
4. Does Cash Flow from Operations exceed Net Profit regularly?
5. Has the company consistently generated Free Cash Flow over the past five years?
6. *Was last year's income tax rate significantly lower than the statutory rate?*

# INDEX

**A**

Accounts Receivables to Sales 297-98, 300
Acquisitions 56, 68, 70, 74-76, 79-80, 84, 136, 152, 158-159, 187, 272, 274, 308, 332, 373
   M&A 71, 74-76, 80, 266, 332
   Serial Acquirers 75, 152, 332
Adaptability 38, 154, 163, 182
Airbnb 202
Alibaba 37
Amazon 37, 159, 167, 184, 310
Andreessen, Marc 195
Apple 164, 166-167
Asset-Light 147, 150-51, 380
Assets to Equity 244, 288, 389

**B**

Base Case 333, 335, 363, 367-368
Bear Case 335, 337, 363, 367-368
Bezos, Jeff 184
Blackberry 164
Board Leadership 22, 34, 127, 129
Bonus 72-73, 102-105, 107-108, 113-115, 225, 377
Branson, Richard 224
Buffett, Warren 36, 72, 75, 98, 131, 136, 199, 215, 313, 315-316, 321, 324, 331
Bull Case 363, 367-368
Business Passion 21, 34, 36, 38, 45-46, 48
Business Scalability 22, 143, 145-148, 150-151, 154, 168, 201, 253 380
Business-Savvy 127, 129, 136-138, 379
Buybacks 76, 80-81, 266, 325

**C**

Capital Allocation 34-35, 68-70, 77-78, 80, 119, 123-124, 152, 374
Capital Expenditures (CAPEX) 150, 274-275, 281-282
Carnegie, Andrew 92
Cash Holding 313-314
Cash Runway Analysis 283
Channel Checks 345-346, 349
Checklist 15-24, 27, 35, 38, 49, 70, 89, 103, 117, 129, 147, 149, 158, 173, 188, 196, 206, 217, 238, 249, 258, 264, 276, 284, 288, 299, 349
Coca-Cola 152
Commodity 65, 172, 185, 204, 206, 208, 287, 384
Common Equity Tier 1 Capital (CET1) 288-289, 389
Competitive Moat 22, 66, 144, 185, 188, 193, 199, 383
   *Brand Loyalty* 63-64, 66, 184, 193, 202

*Network Effects* 63, 193, 201-202
*Process Power* 64, 193, 200-201
*Scale Economies* 64, 193, 199, 201
*Special Assets* 63, 66, 193, 200
*Switching Costs* 64, 178, 193, 201
Compounders 11, 75, 160, 307, 320-322, 331-335, 367
   *Emerging Compounders* 334-335
   *Long-Term Compounders* 331-334, 367
   *M&A Compounders* 75, 332
Compounding 13, 22, 186, 264, 307-309, 312, 316-321, 324, 328, 343
Controlling Owner 117, 121-122, 124, 378
Conviction 18, 27, 45, 160, 320-322, 330-331, 338, 368
Corporate Governance 34-35, 83, 103, 106, 116, 118, 127, 130, 133
   *Governance Committee* 135
Corporate Strategy 38-39, 41, 43, 48-49, 53-55, 61-66, 75-76, 83, 93, 96, 129, 136, 147, 152-153, 161, 196, 221, 226-227, 256, 349, 374, 380
   *Counter-Positioning Strategy* 66-67
Corporate Sustainability 227, 229
Cost Advantages 199
Cost of Capital 126, 188, 192, 260, 357-358, 383
Cost of Debt 357-358, 360-361
Cost of Equity 357-358, 360-361
Cost of Goods Sold (COGS) 247
Culture 54, 56, 80, 92-93, 98, 103, 133, 152, 163, 215, 224
Customer Base 43, 51, 58, 62, 190, 206
Cyclical Business 85, 212-213, 254, 269, 279, 300, 330, 365

**D**

Darwin, Charles 39
Debt to Equity 244, 273, 276, 279, 389
Decentralised 224
Deep-Value Special Situations 331, 335-338
Deposit Growth 288, 294, 389
Discount Rate 24, 355, 357, 368-369
Discounted Cash Flow (DCF) 357, 363
Disruption 66, 152, 156-157, 167-169, 196
Diversification 329, 339
Dividends 68, 70, 80, 83-85, 186, 246, 263-264, 274, 280, 375

**E**

Earnings Before Interest and Taxes (EBIT) 247, 249, 251-253, 255, 273, 276, 280, 387, 389
Earnings Growth 83-85, 262, 264, 268-270, 295, 309-310, 355
Earnings Power 23, 234-235, 238, 240, 310, 336
Earnings Quality 234, 295, 299
eBay 202
Efficiency Ratio, 256-259, 297, 387
Einstein, Albert 316
ESG Analysis 35
Execution Capability 21, 34, 48-49
Executive Compensation 21, 34-35, 102-103, 106, 226-227
Exit Strategy 46

**F**

Financial Health 22, 234, 247, 272, 276, 284, 287-288
Financial Institutions 244, 256, 258-259, 287-294, 389
Fisher, Philip 12, 54, 321, 329, 333, 346-347
Fixed Assets 151, 187
Founder 37, 41, 44, 46, 77-78, 117, 123, 125-126, 184, 214, 220
   *Refounder* 77, 123
Franklin, Benjamin 26
Free Cash Flow (FCF) 99, 145, 247, 253, 274-276, 278, 284-285, 299, 303, 389-390

Freeman-Shore, Lee 326

## G

Geographic Distribution 206
Getty, Paul 321
Google 37, 219
Graham, Benjamin 321
Greenblatt, Joel 13, 330-331
Growth Rate 23, 159, 168, 176, 190, 234-235, 260-262, 264, 266-268, 270, 366, 388

## H

Helmer, Hamilton 67
Human Rights 217, 229

## I

IKEA 10, 37
Incentives 35, 70, 72-73, 103, 109-110, 120, 226, 347, 377
  *Incentive Program* 70, 110
  *Incentive Plan* 59, 70-73, 109, 113-114, 226-227, 375
Independent Directors 129, 131, 379
Insider 119-120, 124, 126, 139, 214
Intangible Assets 151, 187, 281, 291
Intellectual Property 151
Interest Coverage Ratio 273, 280, 360
Inventory to Sales 297, 299
Investment Strategy 11-12, 23, 84, 109, 314, 318-319, 333
Investor Communication 34, 87, 89
  *Shareholder Communication* 87, 90, 94, 97
Investor Responsiveness 89, 100, 376

## K

Kahneman, Daniel 367
Key Employees 110, 206, 214, 384

## L

Leverage 11, 121, 244, 272, 279, 287-288, 318, 360, 389
  *Operating Leverage* 249, 255, 285, 334, 387
Livermore, Jesse 313
Long Product Cycles 158, 163-164, 366, 381

Low-Cost Provider 64
Lynch, Peter 12-13, 27, 311, 321, 326, 328, 342

## M

Market Leadership 45, 163, 188-189, 383
Market Penetration 159, 364
Market Strategy 184, 189
Market Structure 22, 143, 156, 158, 381
Marketing 62, 173, 184, 229, 259, 382
Marks, Howard 12, 71
Mayer, Christopher 12, 310, 323
Munger, Charles 42, 313-314, 320-321, 329

## N

Net Charge-Off Ratio 288, 293, 389
Net Interest Margin (NIM) 244, 256, 258, 387
Net Profit 151, 236-237, 241-244, 254, 263-264, 284-286, 299, 301-302, 390
Netflix 310
Niche Market 62-63, 76, 189, 324, 334
Nokia 166
Non-Performing Loans 288, 290, 292, 389

## O

Operating Cash Flow (OCF) 151, 244, 273, 276-277, 389
  *Cash Flow from Operations* 273-275, 299, 302, 390
Operational Excellence 64, 69
Operational Risks 22, 144, 204-206, 214
Organic Growth 68, 147, 152, 380
  *Inorganic Growth* 332
Ownership 72, 109, 116-125, 131, 200, 218, 279, 378
Ownership Strength 22, 34-35, 72, 116-117

## P

Pay 71-72, 102-104, 106, 108-111, 113, 115, 117, 119, 131, 223-224, 226, 229, 377
  *Exit Payments* 103, 107-108, 377
  *Payout Ratio* 83-85, 263

Phelps, Thomas 12, 85, 317, 322, 332-333
Pre-Revenue Company 46, 57, 147, 155, 380
Price Advantages 201
Pricing Power 195-198
Product Leadership 63
Product/Market Fit 57, 176
Profit Margin 23, 54, 61, 65, 201, 215, 234, 246, 249, 252-254, 256, 258, 364
    *Gross Profit Margin* 188, 195, 198, 247-250, 383, 387
    *Net Profit Margin* 248-249, 254, 387
    *Operating Profit Margin* 247-249, 251-253, 387
Purpose 217, 220-222, 226, 385

## R

Recurring Revenues 145, 148, 176, 186, 380
Redeye 15, 20, 24, 26, 29, 130, 323, 327-328, 357, 363, 365, 367-368
Regulatory Risk 206, 209-210, 384
Retention Ratio 263-264, 388
Return on Assets (ROA) 235-236, 238-239, 386
Return on Capital (ROC) 72, 186
    *Return on Capital Employed (ROCE)* 99
Return on Equity (ROE) 85, 111, 235-238, 240-245, 332, 386
Return on Invested Capital (ROIC) 161-162, 186-187, 190, 192, 260, 365
Risk Premium 57, 358-359, 361
Risk-Free Rate 359, 361
Rumelt, Richard 62

## S

Salary 72-73, 102, 104, 107-108, 113, 120
Scuttlebutt 346-347
Shareholder-Friendly 94, 100, 109, 111
    *Shareholder-Oriented* 129, 136-138, 379

Shearn, Michael 196
Spotify 37
Stock Liquidity 120, 325, 335, 337
Substitutes 27, 43, 173, 178-179, 282, 342, 382

## T

Taleb, Nassim 13, 119
Tax Rate 187, 299, 304, 358, 390
Tenure 44, 51-52, 69, 71, 77-78, 106, 112, 130-131
Texas Ratio 288, 290, 389
Thiel, Peter 19, 200
Top Picks 20, 323, 326-328, 337
Total Addressable Market (TAM) 159, 200
Twain, Mark 341

## V, W

Valuation 13, 19, 24, 26, 79, 81, 100, 114, 145, 147, 155, 206, 211-212, 229, 253, 268, 271-272, 309-310, 324, 333, 335, 339, 355-356, 358, 363-366, 368-369
Value Proposition 22, 144, 149, 167, 171, 173, 182, 220-221
Value Trap 325, 336-337
Visionary 38-39, 75, 373
Voting Rights 117, 124, 126, 378
Washington Post 312-313
Weighted Average Cost of Capital (WACC) 192, 357-358, 361, 365
Working Capital 151, 187, 218, 274, 302

Printed in Great Britain
by Amazon